TAURUS 2003

Teri King's Astrological Horoscopes for 2003

♉

Taurus

Teri King's complete horoscope for all those whose birthdays fall between 20 April and 20 May

Teri King

Thorsons

Thorsons
An Imprint of HarperCollins*Publishers*
77–85 Fulham Palace Road
Hammersmith, London W6 8JB

The Thorsons website address is: www.thorsons.com

and *Thorsons* are trademarks of
HarperCollins*Publishers* Limited

First published 2002

1 3 5 7 9 10 8 6 4 2

©Teri King 2002

Teri King asserts the moral right to be
identified as the author of this work

A catalogue record for this book
is available from the British Library

ISBN 0 00 714063 0

Printed and bound in Great Britain by
Clays Ltd, St Ives plc

℧

Contents

♉

Taurus
20 April to 20 May

Ruling Planet: **Venus**
Element: **Earth**
Qualities: **Feminine, Negative**
Planetary Principle: **Production**
Primal Desire: **Stability**
Colours: **Pink, Baby Blue**
Jewels: **Emerald, Moss Agate**
Day: **Friday**
Magical Number: **Six**

Famous Taureans
Shirley MacLaine, Al Pacino, Jack Nicholson,
William Shakespeare, Bianca Jagger, Michael Palin,
Glenda Jackson, Stevie Wonder, Gabriela Sabatini,
Pete Townsend, Cher.

♉

Introduction

Astrology has many uses, not least of these is its ability to help us to understand both ourselves and other people. Unfortunately, there are many misconceptions and confusions associated with it, such as that old chestnut – how can a zodiac forecast be accurate for all the millions of people born under one particular sign?

The answer to this is that all horoscopes published in newspapers, books and magazines are, of necessity, of a general nature. Unless an astrologer can work from the date, time and place of your birth, the reading given will only be true for the typical member of your sign.

For instance, let's take a person born on 9 August. This person is principally a subject of Leo, simply because the Sun occupied that section of the heavens known as Leo during 23 July to 22 August.* However, when delving into astrology at its most serious, there are other influences that need to be taken into consideration – for example, the Moon. This planet enters a fresh sign every 48 hours. On the birth date in

* Because of the changing position of the planets, calendar dates for astrological signs change from year to year.

♉

question it may have been in, say, Virgo. And if this were the case it would make our particular subject Leo (Sun representing willpower) and Virgo (Moon representing instincts) or, if you will, a Leo/Virgo. Then again, the rising sign of 'ascendant' must also be taken into consideration. This also changes constantly as the Earth revolves: approximately every two hours a new section of the heavens comes into view – a new sign passes over the horizon. The rising sign is of the utmost importance, determining the image projected by the subject to the outside world – in effect, the personality.

The time of birth is essential when compiling a birth chart. Let us suppose that in this particular instance Leo was rising at the time of birth. Now, because two of the three main influences are Leo, our sample case would be fairly typical of his or her sign, possessing all the faults and attributes associated with it. However, if the Moon and ascendant had been in Virgo then, whilst our subject would certainly display some of the Leo attributes or faults, it is more than likely that for the most part he or she would feel and behave more like a Virgoan.

As if life weren't complicated enough, this procedure must be carried through to take into account all the remaining planets. The position and signs of Mercury, Venus, Mars, Jupiter, Saturn, Uranus, Neptune and Pluto must all be discovered, plus the aspect formed from one planet to another. The calculation and interpretation of these movements by an astrologer will then produce an individual birth chart.

Because the heavens are constantly changing, people with identical charts are a very rare occurrence. Although it is not inconceivable that it could happen, this would mean that the two subjects were born not only on the same date and at the same time, but also in the same place. Should such an incident occur, then the deciding factors as to how these individuals would differ in their approach to life, love, career, financial prospects and so on would be due to environmental and parental influence.

Returning to our hypothetical Leo: our example, with the rising Sun in Leo and Moon in Virgo, may find it useful not only to read up on his or her Sun sign (Leo) but also to read the section dealing with Virgo (the Moon). Nevertheless, this does not invalidate Sun sign astrology. This is because of the great power the Sun possesses, and on any chart this planet plays an important role.

Belief in astrology does not necessarily mean believing in totally determined lives – that we are predestined and have no control over our fate. What it does clearly show is that our lives run in cycles, for both good and bad and, with the aid of astrology, we can make the most of, or minimize, certain patterns and tendencies. How this is done is entirely up to the individual. For example, if you are in possession of the knowledge that you are about to experience a lucky few days or weeks, then you can make the most of them by pushing ahead with plans. You can also be better prepared for illness, misfortune, romantic upset and every adversity.

Astrology should be used as it was originally intended – as a guide, especially to character. In this direction it is invaluable and it can help us in all aspects of friendship, work and romance. It makes it easier for us to see ourselves as we really are and, what's more, as others see us. We can recognize both our own weaknesses and strengths and those of others. It can give us outer confidence and inner peace.

In the following pages you will find: personality profiles; an in-depth look at the year ahead from all possible angles, including numerology; monthly and daily guides; and your Sun sign partner guide.

♉

Used wisely, astrology can help you through life. It is not intended to encourage complacency, since, in the final analysis, what you do with your life is up to you. This book will aid you in adopting the correct attitude to the year ahead and thus maximize your chances of success. Positive thinking is encouraged because this helps us to attract positive situations. Allow astrology to walk hand-in-hand with you and you will increase your chances of success and happiness.

How Does
Astrology Work?

You often hear people say that there is no scientific explanation of astrology. This is not a very scientific thing to say because, in fact, astrological calculations may be explained in a very precise way, and they can be done by anyone with a little practice and some knowledge of the movement of stars and planets. However, the interpretations and conclusions drawn from these observations are not necessarily consistent or verifiable, and, to be sure, predicted events do not always happen. Yet astrology has lasted in our culture for over 3,000 years, so there must be something in it!

So how can we explain that astrology? Well, along with your individual birth sign goes a set of deep-seated characteristics, and an understanding of these can give you fresh insights into why you behave as you do. Reading an astrological interpretation, even if it is just to find out how, say, a new relationship might develop, means that you should think about yourself in a very deep way. But it is important to remember that the stars don't determine your fate. It is up to you to use them to the best advantage in any situation.

Although astrology, like many other 'alternative' subjects such as homoeopathy, dowsing and telepathy cannot completely be explained, there have been convincing experiments to show that it is right far more often than chance would allow. The best-known studies are those of the French statistician, Michel Gauqueline, whose results were checked by a professor at the University of London who declared, grudgingly, that 'there was something in it'.

An important aspect of astrology is to look at how the Sun and the Moon affect that natural world around us, day-in day-out. For instance, the rise and fall of the tides is purely a result of the movement and position of the Moon relative to the Earth. If this massive magnetic pull can move the oceans of the Earth, what does it do to us? After all, we are, on average, over 60 per cent water!

When it comes to the ways in which the Sun may change the world, a whole book could be written about it. The influences we know about include length of day, heat, light, solar storms, and magnetic, ultra-violet and many other forms of radiation. And all this from over 90 million miles away! For example, observation of birds has shown that before migration – governed by the changing length of days – birds put on extra layers of fat, as well as experiencing a nocturnal restlessness shortly before setting off on their travels. I'm not suggesting that we put on weight and experience sleepless nights because of the time of year, but many people will tell you that different seasons affect them in different ways.

Also in the natural world, there is a curious species of giant worm that lives in underground caverns in the South Pacific. Twice a year, as the Sun is rising and the tide is at its highest, these worms come to the surface of the ocean. The inhabitants of the nearby islands consider them a great delicacy! There are so many instances where the creatures of this planet respond to the influences of the Moon and the Sun that it is only sensible to wonder whether the position of other planets also has an effect, even if it is subtler and less easy to identify.

Finally, we come to the question of how astrology might work in predicting future events. As we have seen, the planetary bodies are likely to affect us in all sorts of ways, both physically and mentally. Most often, subtle positions in the planets will make slight changes in our emotional states and, of course, this determines how we behave. By drawing up a chart based on precise birth times, and by using their intuition, some astrologers can make precise observations about how influences in the years ahead are likely to shape the life of an individual. Many people are very surprised at how well an astrologer seems to 'understand' them after reading a commentary on their birth chart!

More strange are the astrologers who appear to be able to predict future events, ages before they happen. The most famous example of all is the 16th-century French astrologer, Nostradamus, who is well-known for having predicted the possibility of world destruction at the end of the last millennium. Don't worry; I think I can cheerfully put everyone's mind at rest by assuring you that the world will go on for a good many years yet. Although Nostradamus certainly made some very accurate predictions in his lifetime, his prophecies for our future are very obscure and are hotly disputed by all the experts. Mind you, it is quite clear that there are likely to be massive changes ahead. It is possible, for instance, that information may come to light about past civilizations and cities, which are now sunk beneath the Mediterranean Sea. This could give us a good idea about how people once lived in the past, and pointers as to how we should live in the future. Try not to fear, dear reader. Astrology is a tool for us to use; if we use it wisely, no doubt we will survive with greater wisdom and with a greater respect for our world and each other.

♉

♉

The Sun in Taurus

You have the kind of strength, courage and stamina that will take you anywhere. In matters of love you are faithful, honest and forthright, and hate to be toyed with. Not only do you like to know where you stand in the present, you also like to have a few guarantees for the future. Emotionally, you are much more sensitive than you appear and have a way of hiding your vulnerability behind a carefully controlled exterior. However, in seeking to keep things to yourself, you sometimes lose out, and your reluctance to reveal your deeper emotions can get in the way of you obtaining the kind of attention you need.

There are moments when your strength undermines you, and to avoid the possibility of rejection you try to avoid recognizing your own needs. At this point, you play at being cool, aloof and non-caring. You find it easier to walk away in intense pain with your head held high than to confront the fact that this kind of caution is killing you. You're so enamoured with the role of 'the strong person' that you run the risk of over-playing the part.

One way to avoid this situation is to let your lover know what you are feeling in the present, and what you expect to

♉

feel in the future. You must learn to set the limits in situations and not to sit back while they are set for you.

You're a person of many resources and have a do-it-yourself attitude. People close to you depend on you for your durability, stability and stamina in the face of severe difficulties. You're respected for your tendency to remain unruffled, regardless of the severity of any storm. At the same time, you're quiet with an earthy kind of charm.

Although you could easily find ways of enjoying wealth, it's not all that important to you. You're one person who knows how to be well off with the rudiments of life. With the right amount of love, you are fortified against the world. You can go out and make things happen rather than waiting for them to be given to you. You are steady, sound and efficient in all that you undertake, and you shine through using your own inner resources. You know how to carve out a place for yourself and make it last. With your combined creativity and sense of purpose, the world is yours. All you have to do is to convince yourself that you deserve it, because you do.

♉

♉

The Year Ahead:
Overview

The position of Pluto in Sagittarius suggests that you will occasionally be overwhelmed by a need to search for the meaning of life. This could become obsessive, so do watch out. What's more, you'll become greatly concerned with your resources, perhaps feeling more insecure than usual. You need to adopt an objective attitude towards yourself, and a certain amount of self-criticism too.

Pluto will become its most negative when it goes into retrograde movement on 23 March. This state of affairs exists until 28 August, whereupon it sees sense once more.

For the remainder of the year Pluto coasts along in Sagittarius, once again bringing a certain amount of strain and stress with people you are financially dependent upon. Don't insist on having your own way.

Neptune will be in Aquarius, and will take up retrograde movement on 16 May. This state of affairs exists until 22 October when it finally reverts to normal movement, and you can push ahead again without worrying too much.

Neptune continues in Aquarius for the rest of the year and during this time you may find that people born under the sign of Pisces can be most useful to you. However, we all have

♉

to remember the fact that this sign is not always reliable, though it often means well. You've been warned.

Uranus will squatting in the airy sign of Aquarius from the beginning of the year until 10 March, when it moves into the water sign of Pisces, where it stays until 14 September. Pisces is the area of your chart devoted to friends and with Uranus thus placed there could be sudden break-ups or unexpected attractions; in fact, where this side to life is concerned anything can happen – and it probably will. Uranus sails back into airy Aquarius on 15 September, stirring up tensions between you and your friends and acquaintances. Someone is going to have to give way and it might as well be you.

Saturn is situated in Gemini for the first half of the year, and is in retrograde movement from 1 January through to 21 February. Up until this date, older people may try to hold you back, but once Saturn resumes direct movement on the 22nd, you can push ahead, please yourself, and do what you know needs to be done. On 4 June, Saturn moves on into Cancer, emphasizing matters relating to travel, especially short journeys, and also to brothers and sisters. It seems that you may find yourself feeling a bit down at this time, but it will soon pass.

Jupiter is in retrograde movement in Leo from the beginning of the year until 3 April. This is the area of your chart devoted to family, home and property matters. For some of you, there could be a delightful addition to the family, whilst others are going more up-market where their home is concerned. But please, don't sign any documents until after 3 April.

Jupiter continues in Leo until 26 August when it moves into Virgo – an earth sign, of course, like you, so this is going to be good news. For some of you there'll be gains in an artistic project, for others it may be that you're taking more holidays and relaxing a little bit more than you usually do – and why shouldn't you? After all, you do work hard.

This trend continues until the end of the year where, in the main, it looks as if you'll be having an extremely good time, with any worries down to a minimum – that's always nice, isn't it?

♉

Career Year

Success for you has got to mean security – in love, money and status. But unlike other signs, you don't feel the need to be in the limelight or boast about your achievements. No, you would prefer a comfy seat behind the scenes, especially if your salary sky-rockets annually!

If it's love you're looking for rather than power, it doesn't have to be a jet-set romance with a millionaire (though it would be nice, of course). All you really want is someone to come home to who will provide emotional comfort and security.

Deep in your consciousness, your success is dependent on your security. You want a lover who will not fall in love with somebody else. You want a boss who will not tell you that you're fired. For anything to be successful, it has to be lasting. Novelty doesn't thrill you; it's endurance that counts and gives you the strength to carry on at all costs.

Venus endows you with a great deal of creativity, and because you are an earth sign, there are vast numbers of professions that could suit you and bring success.

You blossom in practical and business matters, and have a great head for details that others might consider boring. But since you're also highly organized, persistent, and have a strong aptitude for cash matters, you could be anything from an executive to a banker to an accountant. You have a very solid, committed approach to what you do, and like to feel that you're steadily building towards better things.

Since Taureans like to build, architecture is another area that may allow you to show off your creative acumen. However, let us not neglect mentioning those truly earthy occupations like landscaping, forestry, conservation, gardening, bricklaying and civil engineering.

Whatever you do, you do it with patience, tenacity and a sense of structure that is rich in purpose. You may not reach the heights as quickly as your friend Aries does, but each stone you slowly turn over on the way, you will be sure to make your own. Your price is stability, and no matter where you're going, you know that you've got that.

During January, Venus, the planet guiding your career, will be in Scorpio until the 7th. That's the area of your chart which rules your opposite number; you will find people much more helpful than usual, so don't be too proud to ask them for assistance. On the 8th, Venus will be moving into Sagittarius. This is good for those of you who work in big business, possibly as part of a team, and also in banking.

This placing lasts until 5 February when Venus moves into Capricorn, the area of your chart devoted to long-distance travelling and higher education. If you are involved in either of these, push ahead like there's no tomorrow.

During March, Venus enters Aquarius on the 3rd, the area of your chart devoted to work, which should be much more enjoyable at this time. Perhaps you're seeing eye-to-eye with colleagues during this period.

Venus moves into Pisces on 28 March, so a tendency to cooperate with others more than usual exists until this planet

ŏ

moves on into Aries on 22 April. This, of course, is a secretive part of your chart so it's good for those of you who work behind the scenes, or who are involved in any kind of research. Don't expect compliments to be thrown at you though: you're going to have to work hard in order to achieve them.

Venus continues through Aries until 15 May, so be prepared to keep a low profile; this will put you in good stead for the future. On the 16th, Venus will be moving into your own sign of Taurus, where it stays until 9 June. This is one time of the year when you can pull out all the stops and push for what you want like crazy, because you can get it – you really can.

Once Venus moves into Gemini on 10 June, the emphasis is going to be on money – so if you work with the nasty stuff you'll be doing exceptionally well right up until 5 July, when Venus enters the sign of Cancer. Once this happens, you may be asked to travel more than is usually the case for the sake of business. Those of you who speculate, bargain and generally hustle around for business, such as freelance workers, should be doing exceptionally well.

This trend continues until 28 July, after which Venus enters the fiery sign of Leo and the area of your chart devoted to property and businesses that are associated with the home and furnishings, etc. It looks as if you are going to be spending a little bit, but if you go over the top you won't please your partner, I can assure you.

Venus will be entering Virgo on 22 August, the area of your chart devoted to children, creativity and everything that is beautiful in life. Certainly you will do well in all your dealings with young people, i.e., everyone from babies to adults! Venus continues in Virgo until 16 September when it enters Libra and the area of your life devoted to sheer hard slog. Just

♉

for once you're not going to baulk or query this at all, because it looks as if rewards are being dangled in front of your eyes, and you're prepared to do whatever is necessary to get what you want.

Venus moves into your opposite sign of Scorpio on 10 October, so regardless of what you do for a living, other people are going to be helpful and may be asking you to combine business with pleasure from time to time so that they can put projects and ideas to you, because they know that you're someone who can make things happen when you decide to do so.

During November, Venus enters Sagittarius on the 3rd – the area of your chart devoted to big business and, to some degree, relationships with those on a professional level, which are good. On the 27th, Venus moves into Capricorn. This is the area of your chart devoted to foreign matters, so some of you may be going on business trips, which will be extremely fruitful. Those of you who work on the Stock Exchange will be receiving some good news. This trend lasts through to 21 December when Venus moves into Aquarius. That is the zenith point of your chart, so you're keeping a high profile and may find promotion – and certainly cooperation – from clients, bosses and everybody in general. It's quite likely that your partner will be extra pleased with all of your efforts, so you won't be wasting your time.

♉

♉

Money Year

Well, Taurus, when it comes to cash you can be both a spend-thrift and a miser. You are an impulsive shopper who often develops a passion for a variety of things, most of which are expensive! And once you are impassioned, you can say good-bye to any concept of economic sensibility!

With a certain kind of Taurus, bills can accrue that bring creditors knocking at your door. When it's really bad you have a way of refusing to face the issues. Maybe, you'll just make paper aeroplanes out of the bills and send them flying swiftly towards the rubbish. But with the other kind of Taureans, the principles of survival are cemented into your consciousness. Therefore, you pay your bills on time and drive yourself to acquire a savings account, as well as some sound investments that ultimately bring you a nice profit.

Money enables you to feel more in control of your life; it also allows those delicious moments of self-indulgence that you so enjoy and usually deserve. By itself, sitting in the bank, money means nothing more than whatever you decide to do with it. And you have a special way of using it to bring you the kind of magical moments of which you always make the most. However, how will you fare during the year ahead?

♉

Well, at the beginning of January, Venus is in Scorpio and that's the area of your chart devoted to insurance, banking and the like. If you want to make any important moves, such as changing your account from one bank to another, this is the ideal time for doing just that. On the 8th, Venus moves into Sagittarius, and this area of your chart is devoted to foreign affairs, travelling and also, to a degree, your ideals. So push ahead with all these sides to life until 4 February and don't waste any time.

Once Venus gets into Capricorn on 5 February, you are all fired up where your ambitions are concerned. You'll be taking potential clients and maybe even your boss out for dinner. Don't crawl to them too much, otherwise you could lose their respect – which would be a great shame. From 5 February to 2 March, with Venus in Capricorn, entertain as much as you can, mixing business with pleasure, and on all occasions you'll be doing yourself a lot of good.

On 3 March, Venus will be moving into Aquarius where it stays until the 27th. That's the area of your chart devoted to friends, team effort and acquaintances, all of which can help to swell your coffers, so stay alert. On 28 March, Venus will be moving into compassionate Pisces, where it stays until 21 April, and most likely you will be at your most generous and open-hearted. What better time to show your appreciation to others – but don't overdo it.

Venus will be moving into Aries on 22 April and will stay there until 15 May. That, of course, is the secretive area of your chart. Oh dear, what are you getting up to? There's no point in thinking you can bounce cheques or behave in any kind of dishonest fashion because, if you do, you'll become seriously unstuck and will generate bad feeling.

From 16 May to 9 June, Venus will be in your own sign,

which is also the money area to your chart. At this time you could become quite mean, wanting to save as much as possible, perhaps for a special surprise for your loved one, or something for yourself – and why not?

On 10 June, Venus will have moved into Gemini where it stays until 4 July. This is the area of your chart devoted to buying and selling and you could find plenty of bargains at this time, so don't pay over the odds for something that you want. From 5 July through to the 28th, Venus will be in Cancer, the area of your chart devoted to home and family. It looks as if you will be splashing out on improving your surroundings and perhaps entertaining at home too, and why not? After all, you've got style – so let other people see it.

Venus will move into Leo on 29 July, where it stays until 21 August. This is the area of your chart devoted to the good times, matters related to children, casual romance and sports, and all of these somehow or another could help you to swell your bank account, so stay alert. From 22 August to 15 September, Venus continues on into Virgo. People born under this sign will be extremely lucky for you and may help you fill the coffers.

From 16 September to 9 October, Venus is in Libra, the area of your chart devoted to sheer hard slog so, in other words, you're not going to get anything unless you are prepared to put yourself out and work like crazy. However, from 10 October to 2 November, Venus will be in Scorpio, your opposite sign. Because of this you may gain from tips that are passed on from close friends, acquaintances and other people. This is a time when you can do yourself quite a lot of good.

From 3 November until the 26th, Venus will be in Sagittarius; that's the area of your chart devoted to short journeys, which could prove to be lucrative in some way. So if you are asked to travel for the sake of your work then do so, and also pay attention when meeting new people, because they may have some useful tips to hand on. From 27 November to 20 December, Venus will be in Capricorn and monies may come in from legal matters, or matters related to foreign ventures.

From 21 December to the end of the year, Venus remains in Aquarius – the area of your chart devoted to work, your profession and work colleagues. Somehow or other you are likely to gain at this time, so don't hesitate to put forward your bright ideas because somebody's going to be impressed, let me tell you.

♉

ಠ

Love and Sex Year

When it comes to love you have a hard time showing your feelings. You're very vulnerable and fear rejection to the point of obsession. In any relationship you have to know where you stand because being put in an insecure position gives you a great deal of pain. Unlike other signs, which consider most interactions to be casual ones to start with, you have hopes for long-term potential for relationships very early in the game. In your younger years, dependencies developed that tied you into relationships for longer than was appropriate. It's hard for you to abandon the hope that things will improve in the future and that meantime the present misery is not in vain.

However, what are your chances during the year ahead?

Well, during January, your ruling planet, Venus, is in Scorpio for the first week. That's throwing a happy glow over all of your close relationships and some of you may think about making that all-important commitment, so you've picked an ideal time. From 8 January, Venus will be moving into Sagittarius and because of this you may be attracted to those with strange sounding names, foreigners in fact – and why not – you are being open-minded.

ಠ

This state of affairs exists until 5 February when Venus moves into Capricorn. Once this occurs you're not really sure that you want to be tied down; in fact you're stepping out of character and deciding to play the field. No reason why you shouldn't, of course, but do try to avoid hurting other people – that would be a great pity.

Venus continues in Capricorn until 2 March, so the care-free freedom you are experiencing continues, but luckily you will always be able to keep a weather eye on the practical side to life regardless of anything. On 3 March, Venus will be moving into Aquarius, the zenith point of your chart. If you meet anyone special it's going to be through your job or your work, so socialize as much as possible with colleagues – you'll be glad that you did.

This trend continues until 28 March, when Venus will be moving into Pisces. This will emphasize the chances of romance through connections with neighbours, brothers, sisters and friends in general. Don't be too proud to accept their invitations.

From 22 April through to 15 May, Venus will be Aries – not such good news, because this suggests that you're not being open with admirers. In fact, you may be even stringing along a couple of admirers. This may swell your ego, Taurus, but it's not going to do much for your credibility when others find out eventually.

On 16 May, Venus will be entering your own sign. You look good, feel good and think you can conquer the world, especially on a romantic level – and you probably can! So get out and socialize and be your usual charming self, certainly up until 10 June anyway, when Venus will be entering Gemini. By this time you seem to be far more concerned with resources than romance, so hopefully you've got a steady relationship to see you through.

During the first few days of July, Venus continues in Gemini, so although you flirt a bit, you are not really serious about romance. On 5 July, Venus moves into Cancer where it stays until the 28th. Again, this signifies lots of casual relationships and enjoying yourself with friends, but you're not even thinking about finding a mate for life.

From 29 July through to 21 August, Venus is in Leo. This is the time you decide you want to spruce up your house and perhaps entertain at home. You may even introduce an admirer to your family or your parents – they'll be well received. From 22 August, Venus is in Virgo. Therefore, your flirty trend gathers momentum and you may find a casual romance with someone from abroad; perhaps you are introduced by a mutual friend.

From 16 September through to 9 October, Venus is Libra; therefore, if you meet anyone special it will be whilst going about your daily life. But I don't think that there are prospects for anything really spectacular at this time, so don't get your hopes up high.

Through to 2 November, Venus is in Scorpio, so you really don't have to even work hard at your social life. Other people are clamouring for your company and they want to be with you, be seen with you, and make interesting introductions. You're rushed off your feet in the nicest possible way!

On 3 November, Venus moves into Sagittarius. Friends may be trying to matchmake for you at this time. Don't be proud. You don't have to expect to find the love of your life, but it could be an awful lot of fun. On 27 November, Venus is in Capricorn, where it stays until 20 December. You'll be attracted to people who come from very different backgrounds, maybe foreigners, and although relationships won't last for overly long, it will certainly create a certain amount of happiness during this run-up to Christmas.

From 21 December through to the end of the year, Venus is in Aquarius and, of course, this is a sign when literally anything can happen, so prepare yourself for just that. Mind you, getting together with workmates would probably be your best bet and, regardless of the time of the year, be as sociable as you can and you're sure to find romance.

♉

♉

Health and Diet Year

As a Bull, weight is usually a problem for you, isn't it? You simply can't say 'no' when it comes to sweets and desserts. You tend to binge, and if it came to a choice between apple pie with ice cream and a dish of plain strawberries, the latter wouldn't even be in the running. To your mind, food is a panacea for all problems. You have a special fondness for bread and other waist-expanding starches. And sugar just sends your senses reeling.

Regardless of your sex, you can probably cook brilliantly – to the detriment of your diet, of course. You love to hang around the kitchen and would rather receive a new wok than a television. Cooking and eating make you feel cosy, so you like to plan your life around these activities.

You like fine wines and frequently spoil yourself with a special bottle. There's nothing wrong with this, but if you buy a crate of the stuff and over indulge in secret you're heading for problems, if not now, then in the future.

As always with Taurus, it is necessary to keep a sense of proportion. If you can do this, you will have little to worry about.

But what about the year ahead? When are the danger periods?

♉

Well, one of the greedy planets of the zodiac is Mars, and during January up until the 16th, it's coasting along in your opposite number, Scorpio. Trying to restrain your appetite is going to be difficult, unless you are bound and gagged of course! Luckily, once Mars gets into Sagittarius on 17 January, this trend evaporates and you channel your energies into thinking of money-making schemes, which isn't a bad idea at all. At least it will help you to avoid rushing to the fridge and raiding it!

From 17 January and throughout February, Mars will be in Sagittarius. You may be having financial problems at this time and although it isn't a good thing, at least it's taking your mind off food and drink and generally pigging out.

During the first few days in March, with Mars still in Sagittarius, you may still want to raid the fridge, but at least you have a certain amount of control around this time. On 5 March, Mars enters Capricorn, where it stays until 21 April. Fortunately Capricorn will be giving you strength, so that you'll be able resist those starchy foods that you so enjoy. You may even lose some weight – providing you're not thinking about it, of course.

From 22 April until 16 June, Mars will be in Aquarius. There is a suggestion here that once more you're full of ambition and, although you may be using other people in order to further your lifestyle, I don't think they're going to mind too much – it must be a rather nice set of friends.

From 17 June right the way through to 16 December, Mars is in Pisces – the area of your chart devoted to short journeys and mental work. Either of these could produce a certain amount of strain and it's up to you to use some common sense. If you can do that, Taurus, you will end the year quite happily, though you must remember that Mars will move into

Aries on 17 December – wouldn't you know it – just in time for Christmas! Never mind, I think this year you may make a vow to yourself not to pig out too much, and in that way you'll stay hale and hearty.

♉

Numerology Year

In order to discover the number of any year you are interested in, your 'individual year number', first take your birth date, day and month, and add this to the year you are interested in, be it in the past or in the future. As an example, say you were born on 13 August and the year you are interested in is 2003:

```
+      13
+       8
     2003
     2024
```

Then, write down 2 + 0 + 2 + 4 and you will discover this equals 8. This means that your year number is 8. If the number adds up to more than 9, add these two digits together.

You can experiment with this method by taking any year from your past and following this guide to find whether or not numerology works out for you.

The guide is perennial and applicable to all Sun signs: you can look up years for your friends as well as for yourself. Use it to discover general trends ahead, the way you should be

approaching a chosen period and how you can make the most
of the future.

Individual Year Number 1

General Feel
A time for being more self-sufficient and one when you should
be ready to really go for it. All opportunities must be snapped
up, after careful consideration. Also an excellent time for
laying down the foundations for future success in all areas.

Definition
Because this is the number 1 individual year, you will have
the chance to start again in many areas of life. The emphasis
will be upon the new; there will be fresh faces in your life,
more opportunities and perhaps even new experiences. If
you were born on either the 1st, 19th or 28th and were born
under the sign of Aries or Leo then this will be an extremely
important time. It is crucial during this cycle that you be prepared to go it alone, push back horizons and generally open
up your mind. Time also for playing the leader or pioneer
wherever necessary. If you have a hobby which you wish to
turn into a business, or maybe you simply wish to introduce
other people to your ideas and plans, then do so whilst experiencing this individual cycle. A great period too for laying
down plans for long-term future gains. Therefore, make sure
you do your homework well and you will reap the rewards
at a later date.

Relationships
This is an ideal period for forming new bonds, perhaps business relationships, new friends and new loves too. You will be

attracted to those in high positions and with strong personali-
ties. There may also be an emphasis on bonding with people a
good deal younger than yourself. If you are already in a long-
standing relationship, then it is time to clear away the dead
wood between you which may have been causing misunder-
standings and unhappiness. Whether in love or business, you
will find those who are born under the sign of Aries, Leo or
Aquarius far more common in your life, also those born on
the following dates: 1st, 4th, 9th, 10th, 13th, 18th, 19th, 22nd
and 28th. The most important months for this individual year,
when you are likely to meet up with those who have a strong
influence on you, are January, May, July and October.

Career

It is likely that you have been wanting to break free and to
explore fresh horizons in your career and this is definitely a
year for doing so. Because you are in a fighting mood, and
because your decision-making qualities as well as your lead-
ership qualities are foremost, it will be an easy matter for you
to find assistance as well as to impress other people. Major
professional changes are likely and you will also feel more
independent within your existing job. Should you want times
for making important career moves, then choose Mondays or
Tuesdays. These are good days for pushing your luck and
presenting your ideas well. Changes connected with your
career are going to be more likely during April, May, July and
September.

Health

If you have forgotten the name of your doctor or dentist, then
this is the year to start regular checkups. A time too when
people of a certain age are likely to start wearing glasses. The

emphasis seems to be on the eyes. Start a good health regime. This will help you cope with any adverse events that almost assuredly lie ahead. The important months for your own health as well as for loved ones are March, May and August.

Individual Year Number 2

General Feel
You will find it far easier to relate to other people.

Definition
What you will need during this cycle is diplomacy, cooperation and the ability to put yourself in someone else's shoes. Whatever you began last year will now begin to show signs of progress. However, don't expect miracles; changes are going to be slow rather than at the speed of light. Changes will be taking place all around you. It is possible too that you will be considering moving from one area to another, maybe even to another country. There is a lively feel about domesticity and in relationships with the opposite sex too. This is going to be a marvellous year for making things come true and asking for favours. However, on no account should you force yourself and your opinions on other people. A spoonful of honey is going to get you a good deal further than a spoonful of vinegar. If you are born under the sign of Cancer or Taurus, or if your birthday falls on the 2nd, 11th, 20th or 29th, then this year is going to be full of major events.

Relationships
You need to associate with other people far more than is usually the case – perhaps out of necessity. The emphasis is on love, friendship and professional partnerships. The opposite

sex will be much more prepared to get involved in your life than is normally the case. This year you have a far greater chance of becoming engaged or married, and there is likely to be a lovely addition both to your family and to the families of your friends and those closest to you. The instinctive and caring side to your personality is going to be strong and very obvious. You will quickly discover that you will be particularly touchy and sensitive to things that other people say. Further, you will find those born under the sign of Cancer, Taurus and Libra entering your life far more than is usually the case. This also applies to those who are born on the 2nd, 6th, 7th, 11th, 15th, 20th, 24th, 25th or 29th of the month.

Romantic and family events are likely to be emphasized during April, June and September.

Career

There is a strong theme of change here, but there is no point in having a panic attack about that because, after all, life is about change. However, in this particular individual year any transformation or upheaval is likely to be of an internal nature, such as at your place of work, rather than external. You may find your company is moving from one area to another, or perhaps there are changes between departments. Quite obviously then, the most important thing for you to do in order to make your life easy is to be adaptable. There is a strong possibility too that you may be given added responsibility. Do not flinch as this will bring in extra reward.

If you are thinking of searching for employment this year, then try to arrange all meetings and negotiations on Monday and Friday. These are good days for asking for favours or rises too. The best months are March, April, June, August and December. All these are important times for change.

♉

Health

This individual cycle emphasizes stomach problems. The important thing for you is to eat sensibly, rather than go on a crash diet, for example – this could be detrimental. If you are female then you would be wise to have a checkup at least once during the year ahead just to be sure you can continue to enjoy good health. All should be discriminating when dining out. Check cutlery, and take care that food has not been partially cooked. Furthermore, emotional stress could get you down, but only if you allow it. Provided you set aside some periods of relaxation in each day when you can close your eyes and let everything drift away, you will have little to worry about. When it comes to diet, be sure that the emphasis is on nutrition, rather than fighting the flab. Perhaps it would be a good idea to become less weight conscious during this period and let your body find its natural ideal weight on its own. The months of February, April, July and November may show health changes in some way. Common sense is your best guide during this year.

Individual Year Number 3

General Feel

You are going to be at your most creative and imaginative during this time. There is a theme of expansion and growth and you will want to polish up your self-image in order to make the 'big impression'.

Definition

It is a good year for reaching out, for expansion. Social and artistic developments should be interesting as well as profitable and this will help to promote happiness. There will be a strong urge in you to improve yourself – either your image or your reputation or, perhaps, your mind. Your popularity soars through the ceiling and this delights you. Involving yourself with something creative brings increased success plus a good deal of satisfaction. However, it is imperative that you keep yourself in a positive mood. This will attract attention and appreciation of all your talents. Projects which were begun two years ago are likely to be bearing fruit this year. If you are born under the sign of Pisces or Sagittarius, or your birthday falls on the 3rd, 12th, 21st or 30th, then this year is going to be particularly special and successful.

Relationships

There is a happy-go-lucky feel about all your relationships and you are in a flirty, fancy-free mood. Heaven help anyone trying to catch you during the next 12 months: they will need to get their skates on. Relationships are likely to be light-hearted and fun rather than heavy going. It is possible too that you will find yourself with those who are younger than you, particularly those born under the signs of Pisces and Sagittarius, and those whose birth dates add up to 3, 6 or 9. Your individual cycle shows important months for relation-ships are March, May, August and December.

Career

As I discussed earlier, this individual number is one that sug-gests branching out and personal growth, so be ready to take on anything new. Not surprisingly, your career prospects look bright and shiny. You are definitely going to be more ambi-tious and must keep up that positive façade and attract opportunities. Avoid taking obligations too lightly; it is important that you adopt a conscientious approach to all your responsibilities. You may take on a fresh course of learning or look for a new job, and the important days for doing so would be on Thursday and Friday: these are definitely your best days. This is particularly true in the months of February, March, May, July and November: expect expansion in your life and take a chance during these times.

Health

Because you are likely to be out and about painting the town all the colours of the rainbow, it is likely that health problems could come through over-indulgence or perhaps tiredness. However, if you must have some health problems, I suppose these are the best ones to experience, because they are under your control. There is also a possibility that you may get a little fraught over work, which may result in some emotional scenes. However, you are sensible enough to realize they should not be taken too seriously. If you are prone to skin allergies, then these too could be giving you problems during this particular year. The best advice you can follow is not to go to extremes that will affect your body or your mind. It is all very well to have fun, but after a while too much of it affects not only your health but also the degree of enjoyment you experience. Take extra care between January and March, and June and October, especially where these are winter months for you.

Individual Year Number 4

General Feel

It is back to basics this year. Do not build on shaky founda-tions. Get yourself organized and be prepared to work a little

♉

harder than you usually do and you will come through without any great difficulty.

Definition

It is imperative that you have a grand plan. Do not simply rush off without considering the consequences and avoid dabbling of any kind. It is likely too that you will be gathering more responsibility and on occasions this could lead you to feeling unappreciated, claustrophobic and perhaps over-burdened in some ways. Although it is true to say that this cycle in your individual life tends to bring about a certain amount of limitation, whether this be on the personal, the psychological or the financial side of life, you now have the chance to get yourself together and to build on more solid foundations. Security is definitely your key word at this time. When it comes to any project, job or plan, it is important that you ask the right questions. In other words, do your homework and do not rush blindly into anything. That would be a disaster. If you are an Aquarius, a Leo or a Gemini or you are born on the 4th, 13th, 22nd or the 31st of any month, this individual year will be extremely important and long remembered.

Relationships

You will find that it is the eccentric, the unusual, the unconventional and the downright odd who will be drawn into your life during this particular cycle. It is also strongly possible that people you have not met for some time may be re-entering your circle and an older person or somebody outside your own social or perhaps religious background will be drawn to you too. When it comes to the romantic side of life, again you are drawn to that which is different from usual. You may even form a relationship with someone who comes from a totally

ɣ

different background, perhaps from far away. Something unusual about them stimulates and excites you. Gemini, Leo and Aquarius are your likely favourites, as well as anyone whose birth number adds up to 1, 4, 5 or 7. Certainly the most exciting months for romance are going to be February, April, July and November. Make sure then that you socialize a lot during these particular times, and be ready for literally anything.

Career

Once more we have the theme of the unusual and different in this area of life. You may be plodding along in the same old rut when suddenly lightning strikes and you find yourself besieged by offers from other people and, in a panic, not quite sure what to do. There may be a period when nothing particular seems to be going on when, to your astonishment, you are given a promotion or some exciting challenge. Literally anything can happen in this particular cycle of your life. The individual year 4 also inclines towards added responsibilities and it is important that you do not off-load them onto other people or cringe in fear. They will eventually pay off and in the meantime you will be gaining in experience and paving the way for greater success in the future. When you want to arrange any kind of meeting, negotiation or perhaps ask for a favour at work, then try to do so on a Monday or a Wednesday for the luckiest results. January, February, April, October and November are certainly the months when you must play the opportunist and be ready to say yes to anything that comes your way.

♉

Health

The biggest problems that you will have to face this year are
caused by stress, so it is important that you attend to your
diet and take life as philosophically as possible, as well as
being ready to adapt to changing conditions. You are likely to
find that people you thought you knew well are acting out of
character and this throws you off balance. Take care, too,
when visiting the doctor. Remember that you are dealing with
a human being and that doctors, like the rest of us, can make
mistakes. Unless you are 100 per cent satisfied then go for a
second opinion over anything important. Try to be sceptical
about yourself because you are going to be a good deal more
moody than usual. The times that need special attention are
February, May, September and November. If any of these
months falls in the winter part of your year, then wrap up
well and dose up on vitamin C.

Individual Year Number 5

General Feel

There will be many more opportunities for you to get out and
about, and travel is certainly going to be playing a large part
in your year. Change, too, must be expected and even
embraced – after all, it is part of life. You will have more free
time and choices, so all in all things look promising.

Definition

It is possible that you tried previously to get something off the
launchpad, but for one reason or another it simply didn't
happen. Luckily, you now get a chance to renew those old
plans and put them into action. You are certainly going to feel
that things are changing for the better in all areas. You will be

♉

more actively involved with the public and enjoy a certain
amount of attention and publicity. You may have failed in the
past but this year mistakes will be easier to accept and learn
from; you are going to find yourself both physically and mentally more in tune with your environment and with those you
care about than ever before. If you are a Gemini or a Virgo or
are born on the 5th, 14th or 23rd, then this is going to be a
period of major importance for you and you must be ready to
take advantage of this.

Relationships

Lucky you! Your sexual magnetism goes through the ceiling
and you will be involved in many relationships during the
year ahead. You have that extra charisma about you which
will be attracting others and you can look forward to being
choosy. There will be an inclination to be drawn to those who
are considerably younger than yourself. It is likely too that
you will find that those born under the signs of Taurus,
Gemini, Virgo and Libra as well as those whose birth date
adds up to 2, 5 or 6 will play an important part in your year.
The months for attracting others in a big way are January,
March, June, October and December.

Career

This is considered by all numerologists to be one of the best
numbers for self-improvement in all areas, but particularly on
the professional front. It will be relatively easy for you to sell
your ideas and yourself, as well as to push your skills and
expertise under the noses of other people. They will certainly
sit up and take notice. Clearly, then, this is a time for you to
view the world as your oyster and to get out there and grab
your piece of the action. You have increased confidence and

should be able to get exactly what you want. Friday and Wednesday are perhaps the best days if looking for a job or going to negotiations or interviews, or in fact for generally pushing yourself into the limelight. Watch out for March, May, September, October or December. Something of great importance could pop up at this time. There will certainly be a chance for advancement; whether you take it or not is, of course, entirely up to you.

Health

Getting a good night's rest could be your problem during the year ahead, since that mind of yours is positively buzzing and won't let you rest. Try turning your brain off at bedtime, otherwise you will finish up irritable and exhausted. Try to take things a step at a time without rushing around. Meditation may help you to relax and do more for your physical well-being than anything else. Because this is an extremely active year, you will need to do some careful planning so that you can cope with ease rather than rushing around like a demented mayfly. Furthermore, try to avoid going over the top with alcohol, food, sex, gambling or anything which could be described as a 'quick fix'. During January, April, August and October, watch yourself a bit, you could do with some pampering, particularly if these happen to be winter months for you.

Individual Year Number 6

General Feel

There is likely to be increased responsibility and activity within your domestic life. There will be many occasions when you will be helping loved ones and your sense of duty is going to be strong.

Definition

Activities for the most part are likely to be centered around property, family, loved ones, romance and your home. Your artistic appreciation will be good and you will be drawn to anything that is colourful and beautiful, and possessions that have a strong appeal to your eye or even your ear. Where domesticity is concerned, there is a strong suggestion that you may move out of one home into another. This is an excellent time, too, for self-education, for branching out, for graduating, for taking on some extra courses – whether simply to improve your appearance or to improve your mind. When it comes to your social life you are inundated with chances to attend events. You are going to be a real social butterfly, flitting from scene to scene and enjoying yourself thoroughly. Try to accept nine out of ten invitations that come your way because they bring with them chances of advancement. If you are born on the 6th, 15th or 24th, or should your birth sign be Taurus, Libra or Cancer, then this year will be long remembered as a very positive one.

Relationships

When it comes to love, sex and romance the individual year 6 is perhaps the most successful. It is a time for being swept off your feet, for becoming engaged or even getting married. On the more negative side, perhaps, there could be separation and divorce. However, the latter can be avoided, provided you are prepared to sit down and communicate properly. There is an emphasis too on pregnancy and birth, or changes in existing relationships. Circumstances will be sweeping you along. If you are born under the sign of Taurus, Cancer or Libra, then it is even more likely that this will be a major year for you, as well as for those born on dates adding up to 6, 3

♉

or 2. The most memorable months of your year are going to be February, May, September and November. Grab all opportunities to enjoy yourself and improve your relationships during these periods.

Career
A good year for this side of life too, with the chances of promotion and recognition for past efforts all coming your way. You will be able to improve your position in life even though it is likely that recently you have been disappointed. On the cash front, big rewards will come flooding in mainly because you are prepared to fulfil your obligations and commitments without complaint or protest. Other people will appreciate all the efforts you have put in, so plod along and you will find your efforts will not have been in vain. Perversely, if you are looking for a job or setting up an interview, negotiation or a meeting, or simply want to advertise your talents in some way, then your best days for doing so are Monday, Thursday and Friday. Long-term opportunities are very strong during the months of February, April, August, September and November. These are the key periods for pushing yourself up the ladder of success.

Health
If you are to experience any problems of a physical nature during this year, then they could be tied up with the throat, nose or the tonsils, plus the upper parts of the body. Basically, what you need to stay healthy during this year is plenty of sunlight, moderate exercise, fresh air and changes of scene. Escape to the coast if this is at all possible. The months for being particularly watchful are March, July, September and December. Think twice before doing anything during these

times and there is no reason why you shouldn't stay hale and hearty for the whole year.

Individual Year Number 7

General Feel

A year for inner growth and for finding out what really makes you tick and what you need to make you happy. Self-awareness and discovery are all emphasized during the individual year 7.

Definition

You will be provided with the opportunity to place as much emphasis as possible on your personal life and your own well-being. There will be many occasions when you will find yourself analysing your past motives and actions, and giving more attention to your own personal needs, goals and desires. There will also be many occasions when you will want to escape any kind of confusion, muddle or noise; time spent alone will not be wasted. This will give you the chance to meditate and also to examine exactly where you have come to so far, and where you want to go in the future. It is important you make up your mind what you want out of this particular year because once you have done so you will attain those ambitions. Failure to do this could mean you end up chasing your own tail and that is a pure waste of time and energy. You will also discover that secrets about yourself and other people could be surfacing during this year. If you are born under the sign of Pisces or Cancer, or on the 7th, 16th or 25th of the month, then this year will be especially wonderful.

ඊ

Relationships

It has to be said from the word go that this is not the best year for romantic interest. A strong need for contemplation will mean spending time on your own. Any romance that does develop this year may not live up to your expectations, but, providing you are prepared to take things as they come without jumping to conclusions, then you will enjoy yourself without getting hurt. Decide exactly what it is you have in mind and then go for it. Romantic interests this year are likely to be with people who are born on dates that add up to 2, 4 or 7, or with people born under the sign of Cancer or Pisces. Watch for romantic opportunities during January, April, August and October.

Career

When we pass through this particular individual cycle, two things in life tend to occur: retirement from the limelight, and a general slowing down, perhaps by taking leave of absence or maybe retraining in some way. It is likely too that you will become more aware of your own occupational expertise and skills – you will begin to understand your true purpose in life and will feel much more enlightened. Long-sought-after goals begin to come to life if you have been drifting of late. The best attitude to have throughout this year is an exploratory one when it comes to your work. If you want to set up negotiations, interviews or meetings, arrange them for Monday or Friday. In fact, any favours you seek should be tackled on these days. January, March, July, August, October and December are particularly good for self-advancement.

♉

Health

Since, in comparison with previous years, this is a rather quiet time, health problems are likely to be minor. Some will possibly come through irritation or worry and the best thing to do is to attempt to remain meditative and calm. This state of mind will bring positive results. Failure to do so may create unnecessary problems by allowing your imagination to run completely out of control. You need time this year to restore, recuperate and contemplate. Any health changes that do occur are likely to happen in February, June, August and November.

Individual Year Number 8

General Feel

This is going to be a time for success, for making important moves and changes, a time when you may gain power and certainly one when your talents are going to be recognized.

Definition

This individual year gives you the chance to 'think big'; it is a time when you can occupy the limelight and wield power. If you were born on the 8th, 17th or 26th of the month or come under the sign of Capricorn, pay attention to this year and make sure you make the most of it. You should develop greater maturity and discover a true feeling of faith and destiny, both in yourself and in events that occur. This part of the cycle is connected with career, ambition and money, but debts from the past will have to be repaid. For example, an old responsibility or debt that you may have avoided in past years may reappear to haunt you. However, whatever you do with these 12 months, aim high – think big, think success and above all be positive.

♉

Relationships

This particular individual year is one which is strongly connected with birth, divorce and marriage – most of the land-
marks we experience in life, in fact. Love-wise, those who are
more experienced or older than you, or people of power,
authority, influence or wealth, will be very attractive. This year
will be putting you back in touch with those from your past
– old friends, comrades, associates, and even romances
from long ago crop up once more. You should not experience
any great problems romantically this year, especially if you
are dealing with Capricorns or Librans, or with those
whose date of birth adds up to 8, 6 or 3. The best months for
romance to develop are likely to be March, July, September
and December.

Career

The number 8 year is generally believed to be the best one
when it comes to bringing in cash. It is also good for asking
for a rise or achieving promotion or authority over other
people. This is your year for basking in the limelight of success, the result perhaps of your past efforts. Now you will be
rewarded. Financial success is all but guaranteed, provided
you keep faith with your ambitions and yourself. It is important that you set major goals for yourself and work slowly
towards them. You will be surprised how easily they are
fulfilled. Conversely, if you are looking for work, then do
set up interviews, negotiations and meetings, preferably on
Saturday, Thursday or Friday, which are your luckiest days.
Also watch out for chances to do yourself a bit of good during
February, June, July, September and November.

♉

Health

You can avoid most health problems, particularly headaches, constipation or liver problems, by avoiding depression and feelings of loneliness. It is important when these descend that you keep yourself busy enough not to dwell on them. When it comes to receiving attention from the medical profession you would be well advised to get a second opinion. Eat wisely, try to keep a positive and enthusiastic outlook on life and all will be well. Periods which need special care are January, May, July and October. Therefore, if these months fall during the winter part of your year, wrap up well and dose yourself with vitamins.

Individual Year Number 9

General Feel

A time for tying up loose ends. Wishes are likely to be fulfilled and matters brought to swift conclusions. Inspiration runs amok. Much travel is likely.

Definition

The number 9 individual year is perhaps the most successful of all. It tends to represent the completion of matters and affairs, whether in work, business or personal affairs. Your ability to let go of habits, people and negative circumstances or situations, that may have been holding you back, is strong. The sympathetic and humane side to your character also surfaces and you learn to give more freely of yourself without expecting anything in return. Any good deeds that you do will certainly be well rewarded in terms of satisfaction, and perhaps financially, too. If you are born under the sign of

Aries or Scorpio, or on the 9th, 18th or 27th of the month, this is certainly going to be an all-important year.

Relationships

The individual year 9 is a cycle which gives appeal as well as influence. Because of this, you will be getting emotionally tied up with members of the opposite sex who may be outside your usual cultural or ethnic group. The reason for this is that this particular number relates to humanity and of course this tends to quash ignorance, pride and bigotry. You also discover that Aries, Leo and Scorpio people are going to be much more evident in your domestic affairs, as well as those whose birth dates add up to 9, 3 or 1. The important months for relationships are February, June, August and November. These will be extremely hectic and eventful from a romantic viewpoint and there are times when you could be swept off your feet.

Career

This is a year which will help to make many of your dreams and ambitions come true. Furthermore, it is an excellent time for success if you are involved in marketing your skills, talents and expertise more widely. You may be thinking of expanding abroad for example and, if so, this is certainly a good idea. You will find that harmony and cooperation with your fellow workers are easier than before and this will help your dreams and ambitions. The best days for you if you want to line up meetings or negotiations are going to be Tuesdays and Thursdays, and this also applies if you are looking for employment or want a special day for doing something of an ambitious nature. Employment or business changes could also feature during January, May, June, August and October.

♉

Health

The only physical problems you may have during this particular year will be because of accidents, so be careful. Try, too,
to avoid unnecessary tension and arguments with other
people. Take extra care when you are on the roads: no drinking and driving, for example. You will only have problems if
you play your own worst enemy. Be extra careful when in the
kitchen or bathroom: sharp instruments that you find in these
areas can lead to cuts, unless you take care.

♉

♉

Your Sun Sign Partner

Taurus with Taurus

It seems the longer you two stick together, the longer you stay in the same place. At first sight, this is the most secure situation. However, on reflection, it signifies the worst kind of ennui, and can lead to sedentary stagnation.

This is a relationship in which nothing ever seems to happen, because both of you are patiently waiting for the command. After a while, life starts to get like a 2 a.m. TV movie with too many commercials.

What really cements you two together is the stability of inertia. However, it is only years later, at a point of jaundiced indifference, that you will actually admit that the only stability is via change.

Taurus Woman

Taurus Woman with Aries Man
He's so pushy, but she is placid. He's impatient, but she just waits for change. He's flighty, and she never gets off the ground. But the very worst is that he's so bossy that

sometimes she just wants to bribe him to shut up.

He sees himself as very exciting and will tell her all about it. But what he won't tell her is that he has a temper that could make her swallow her chewing gum.

He lives for challenges, whereas she needs stability. He is freedom loving, whilst she is fearful of moments spent alone. He's a many woman man, but she is a one man woman. Basically he's looking for fireworks, whilst she is satisfied with just a little warmth.

Taurus Woman with Gemini Man

She embraces stability; he can't exist without change. She gives her life towards future security, while he can't think past the present second. She gravitates towards a quiet kind of evening; he prefers the New Year celebrations.

Needless to say, this combination is not the most compatible. She needs someone steady, and he is maddeningly capricious. He wants a woman with a mind like a quiz show and she wants to be loved for what she is.

He'll stand her up, forget her phone number and maybe even her first name. With him, there's only one thing that she can rely on – the fact that he is utterly unreliable.

Taurus Woman with Cancer Man

Much passion will definitely pass between these two. But whether the relationship lasts depends upon where they both want to take it.

He is loyal and loving, but the meaning of his moods will totally elude her. One moment he is insecure and dependent and another, he is totally withdrawn. Feelings have a way of tying the two of them up in knots. Together, they will satiate each other's security needs. However, she is the more practical

♉

one, he the more passionate. She is the earthy foundation; he is the ivory tower.

Taurus Woman with Leo Man

She is security oriented – both materially and emotionally. So if he buys her daffodils, takes her to a posh restaurant, and over the peach melba croons 'It had to be you', suddenly she'll be his and may even forget to eat her ice cream. However, he should join a health club immediately, since she'll already be planning his menus.

She loves to nurture and to be nurtured. Hence, even the plants have come to think of her as Mother. Domestic duties that bore him seem to delight her. However, before he sits back and wonders when dinner will be ready, he should keep in mind the handy little fact that nothing in this world is free, and she too has a price – it's called marriage.

Taurus Woman with Virgo Man

Although he may nag her about the bathtub ring, she'll find this man endearing. He's honest, vulnerable, giving and loving. Because he tends to be a quiet stay-at-home type, together they can share many cosy evenings. A flickering fire, some fillet mignon and a carafe of Beaujolais and they're both on their way to heaven.

She'll find him considerate, and he will find her warm and caring. He appreciates her practicality. She appreciates the competence with which he runs his life. He tends to be shy, but she can melt his inhibitions with her animal sensuality.

Taurus Woman with Libra Man

She'll think she's really 'in' when he begins all his sentences with 'we'. However, she should listen longer: she still needs

♉

to hear those little words – 'I love you'. But she shouldn't be surprised if she finds herself smoking, eating, waiting and listening.

Basically, he wants to hear bells ring and feel the earth move, whilst she's content to sacrifice the sound effects for some stability and solid ground. However, with Mr Libra, she'll only be treading in the cracks. He's not one to lean on, nor is he the one to soothe her insecurities. On the contrary, he may confirm them and create new ones.

Taurus Woman with Scorpio Man

He'll take her to his bosom and make her travel places that she'd never even thought of before. In the course of just one day, she will find him alluring, mysterious, magnetic, sexy and dangerous. He is – and he's very glad that she has the intelligence to know it.

He'll find her warm, sensual, domestic, insecure and very vulnerable. He can see through her lovingly prepared strawberry cheesecakes straight into her soul, and what he'll see is a tremendous sense of need and a longing to be needed. At first, this may frighten him, and during the dessert he may consider how best to make his excuses and leave. However, something besides the second cup of coffee and Grand Marnier will make him stay. He has no idea what it really is, and that's because it is a combination of many different things.

For her this partnership is a fatal attraction. Her heart will get caught up in his contradictions, and he'll enjoy the power he has watching her try to escape. She is like a fly trapped in a spider's web. But to her mind, Mr Scorpio is a kind of three-ringed circus without sound. She never knows what show goes on next, and half the time she's no idea what she's

♉

watching. What he does and says and desires and wants and hates and needs is all beyond her. From her perspective the workings of his mind are more obscure than the Bible translated into Chinese.

Her greatest desire is an honest relationship without games, and the kind of passion that comes without pain. He finds such scenes comforting only when he feels sad and lonely. At all other times, he wants his attention to be galvanized by some sort of challenge. Because of this, in the long run, he may leave her feeling cold and hungry.

Therefore, the outcome of this meeting is most likely to be of one of two people who pass in the night. If she's smart, the first thing she should do when she sees him is just keep on walking – if not running. In this way she'll save herself a lot of heartache.

Taurus Woman with Sagittarius Man

He is a man of adventure, while she is a cosy stay-at-home. He likes to battle with the elements, while she likes to watch the world from a four-poster bed. She is attached to her creature comforts while he runs around and loves to rough it.

He is a fanatic for every kind of sport and has a hard time sitting still when he's eating. She prefers a sedentary lifestyle, and keeps all athletics restricted to the bedroom. His sense of humour overshadows every situation. His idea of romance is to arm wrestle, whilst hers is to sniff peonies while wearing silk.

Taurus Woman with Capricorn Man

He is the archetypal ambitious breadwinner, and the kind of man she would like to take command. She is the archetypal fertile earth mother, and the kind of woman he would like to serve.

♉

These two share a sense of practicality and purpose that will truly draw them together. He is responsible, dutiful, loyal and loving. She is solid, stable, devoted and nurturing.

She admires his ambitious hard-working nature. He respects her resourcefulness and understands her security needs. Together they could build a business, a marriage, a family or a corporation.

Taurus Woman with Aquarius Man
He is far more interested in what's out in space than in what's right in front of him. And when it comes to those little sensual pleasures that make her life worth living, he has a way of reducing them all to nothing.

He'll torment her possessive proclivities and put her jealousy through a kind of trial by fire. Communication between the two is like an Arab eating pasta with a Russian. All that comes through are the strangest sounds.

His deepest desire is to have wings, whilst hers is to have an anchor. He is attached to non-attachment, whilst she has an infinite capacity for devotion. He sees love as merely an idea, while she sees it as the stuff that life is made of. He considers the perfect connubial commitment to be an open marriage, whilst she would love a husband whom she can lock up.

Needless to say, this is not a very compatible partnership.

Taurus Woman with Pisces Man
He is a fantasy addict, while she prefers facing the facts. If she marries him she'll be taking on the responsibility of a caretaker in a home for convalescents.

He can't be bothered with day-to-day details, so she has to assume what he shuns. He's overflowing with sympathy for the under-privileged. However, should she develop an acute

♉

case of bronchial pneumonia, he'll still expect her to take the car in for its yearly service. Undoubtedly he will feel that she is a fine person, but the problem is that he thinks that about every woman he meets.

Taurus Man

Taurus Man with Aries Woman

He won't exactly appreciate the way she points when she wants something. She won't like the way he refuses to move when she points.

This woman is bossy and is used to wrapping men around her little finger and squeezing hard. Although he would be willing to climb Everest for some lady who asked him nicely, he doesn't at all appreciate the pushy touch.

Sexually, she is his match; however, she just may be other men's as well. Basically, she does not believe in Mr Right, and therefore is always open to the most casual affairs. She is adventurous, while he loathes risk taking. She is committed to the moment, while he is ready to sell his soul for the future.

Taurus Man with Gemini Woman

She is freedom loving and flippant; he is security oriented and serious. She loves to test and tease and at any given moment has a thousand little games up her sleeve. As he can only deal with a home-loving woman or one who lays all her cards face up on the table, she is enough to give him a psychosomatic case of lockjaw.

At best this relationship should be confined to that of bank manager and customer, where he can help her with her bounced cheques and sort out her overdraft.

ಠ

Taurus Man with Cancer Woman

These two are truly stay-at-home creatures and can have a lovely evening just cooking a cabbage quiche. At times she will remind him of his mother on Christmas morning. He will remind her of Daddy and days when he paid the rent.

In each other they find security: fantasies are satisfied and for both of them that is a lot. She will find he is someone solid to lean on, while he will find her a cushion of kindness.

Taurus Man with Leo Woman

This is definitely not a match made in heaven, as both have a will that could splinter steel. He is stubborn and rigid; she is defiant and stubborn. Combined, these inharmonious qualities can spell heartache.

He prefers to stay at home, while she wears holes in the floor if she can't get out. She likes the drama and excitement of life while he will be content with the 10 o'clock news.

It's not unlikely that he could outdo her in the kitchen – a quality she greatly appreciates since she never considered it a divine right to have to cook. Yet, when he's slaved away for hours over the stove to create a 10-course meal, and she dawdles over the asparagus because she's dieting, things can become decidedly frosty.

Taurus Man with Virgo Woman

She'll clean up when he has made a mess. He'll cook for her when she's tired. Together they can build a bastion of love where both can gain the nurturing they need. He admires her neatness and the way she respects her body. She admires his emotional strength, and marvels at his stamina and endurance.

♉

In terms of marriage, these two are a team that is mar-velled at, since their relationship seems to have a stability that looks too good to be true. This is because they are both so solid. Just remember to make the most of it.

Taurus Man with Libra Woman

This could be romance at second sight. She has the sense of beauty he admires and he has the money to buy the beauty she desires.

Emotionally, she is so up and down that she'll fall in love with him just because he never gets depressed. He is a rock of stability while she is wishy-washy; she is an airy romantic and he is a practical idealist. He'll take care of her moods by buying her trinkets and smothering her with love. She'll satisfy his desires by cooking him a dinner that sends him into a swoon.

She needs someone with strong arms and he is just the person who can imprison her. At the same time, he needs a woman who knows how to learn.

Taurus Man with Scorpio Woman

Chances are she won't find this chemistry a delight, unless he's cooking her dinner. And he'll probably do that only because he's too cheap to take her out. If she breaks her tooth on the bread, it's undoubtedly because it was reduced for a quick sale. And if the milk in her coffee separates, it's only because he wanted to use up last week's before he opened a new bottle. And should the steak have muscles stronger than hers after six months of jogging, she'll know that he haggled with the discount butcher.

He goes into ruts more often than any other sign, so if she wants to get rid of him for good, she will have to dig him another and then give him a push forward.

♉

Taurus Man with Sagittarius Woman
Her idea of fun is lots of physical activity; his idea of physical activity is either sex or over-eating.

She'll get up at dawn just to work on her backhand, while he would rather spend the day eating pasta than playing tennis. She loves to travel from country to country, while he rarely moves from room to room. She prefers a Spartan lifestyle to the lap of luxury. He prefers a 5-star hotel to roughing it.

Needless to say, it is highly unlikely that these two will bring each other a lifetime of untarnished bliss. Instead, he will be better off returning to his simmering pot of ragout while she goes on a solitary shopping spree for some new sweat bands.

Taurus Man with Capricorn Woman
She'll find him better than a Christmas present on a rainy morning. He'll find her to be the kind of competent career woman he's always had a crush on.

She is strong and dignified yet with a lot of feeling underneath a cool surface. He is warm and cuddly with an earthiness that makes her feel at ease. Together they will linger over the steak Diane in the candle glow and he will find her so stimulating that he may lose his appetite and not stop for an ice cream on the way home.

If anything, Ms Capricorn will probably make him go on a diet. So he'd better clean out his frozen pizzas, have a party, and announce to the world that he's fallen in love.

Taurus Man with Aquarius Woman
She tends towards humanitarian impulses, while his impulses are of a more self-seeking kind. She is independent and

interested in everything around her, while he is more dependent and interested in what immediately concerns her. She
likes to spread her time among a thousand people, while he
prefers to concentrate on just a few.

He tends either to hoard his money or to spend it self
indulgently. She likes to give hers away to needy people. She
gets carried away by good causes, while the greatest cause he
embraces is personal gain. He gravitates towards the material,
while her needs tend to be ethereal. It was someone just like
him who created management and it was someone just like
her who created revolutionary uprising.

A communication gap here is like a cosmic crack in the
universe. If he hangs around her too long, he may just fall in.

Taurus Man with Pisces Woman

He is like a big house that she can lean against, and only a
Taurus man could stand the weight. She is fragile, vulnerable
and with a mental make-up that he will never understand. He
is a solid force with a matter-of-fact philosophy that totally
eludes her because it's so simple.

The compatibility here is not exactly attention grabbing –
however, the underlying needs that are satisfied are something else. Both tend to be enslaved by the sensual pleasures
that quicken the pulse. Both like to sleep in the sun and open
their eyes to fresh orange juice spiked with a little vodka. Both
adore marathon sex from dawn until dusk. And both prefer a
body that is naked to one that is nicely dressed. At this point
the similarities start to dwindle. She's emotional and weepy,
while he is practical and puts his emotions in a place where
they don't show. Her sacred dwelling is in daydreams while
his is in a material dynasty rooted in earth.

℧

He finds her seductive, alluring and at times more mysterious than his mind can take. She finds him solid, stubborn, sensual and someone she can depend on. Together they could become a good team, if their divergent approaches to life don't get seriously in the way.

♉

♉

Monthly and Daily Guides

JANUARY

During January the Sun will be drifting along in the earthy sign of Capricorn until the 19th. This is the area of your chart associated with higher education, long-distance travel and matters related to abroad; therefore, if you have friends or contacts in foreign climes, you're likely to be hearing from them. Furthermore, you could be very idealistic at this time, but you've got to remember that unless you are perfect you have no right to expect such behaviour from other people.

On the 20th, the Sun moves into Aquarius, the zenith point of your chart, so the ambitious side to your character begins to surface and heaven help anybody who gets in your way. Try to remember, though, that you mustn't neglect those at home or bore them with stories about your work – it's OK if something exceptional is happening, but they really won't want a blow-by-blow report on your professional life.

Mercury will be in the earthy sign of Capricorn all month and will also be in retrograde movement for most of the

♉

month, so do take care when dealing with people who come from different lands. You could be tactless and say the wrong thing at the wrong time. There's no harm in the Bull, of course, but even so a little bit of caution is certainly going to take you a long way.

Luckily, Mercury finally resumes direct movement on the 23rd, so after this date you can travel, sign documents and generally make little changes without fear of doing the wrong thing.

Venus is in Scorpio for the first week of January and that, of course, is your opposite sign. This does throw a rosy glow over all of your relationships and if you have been involved with somebody for quite some time, you may be even considering naming the day. For others, you might just use this as an excuse for getting out and about and thoroughly enjoying yourself – and why shouldn't you?

On 8 January, Venus will be moving into Sagittarius and the area of your chart devoted to work, legal matters and shared resources over which there seems to be a good positive feel. So push ahead with these areas to life because basically you have nothing to lose. Venus remains in this sign till the end of the month and beyond.

Mars will be in Scorpio until the 16th and you will find that other people are suffering from strains and stresses. There's no point in expecting any favours from them: you're going to be unlucky, so don't even bother to ask.

On 17 January, Mars moves into Sagittarius where it stays for the remainder of the month. That's the area of your chart devoted to sheer hard slog, as well as insurance matters and perhaps secret deep feelings.

In the main, the stars seem to be on your side, with only one or two little hiccups.

♉

1 WEDNESDAY This is a rather miserable season of the year and it's not unlikely that you, and indeed many other signs, may be thinking of summer holidays – well it helps us get through these miserable days and nights, doesn't it? In your case though, you may leap into action and book a holiday without consulting your partner, which won't go down well, so make sure that you do discuss it.

2 THURSDAY There's a bright New Moon today in the sign of Capricorn. Once more you're yearning for change and for distant shores. If you have any foreigners in your circle they are the ones to go to if you need any kind of advice or help. They'll be only too glad to be of service, but then again that's what friendship is for, isn't it?

3 FRIDAY Narrow-minded friends are the least of your worries. Don't give up a heavenly outing for the sake of someone else's whims. Persist, and go where you want - you might end up in Paradise. The last thing you need to do is to be weighed down by people telling you how you should be pulling out all the stops. You know exactly how to handle your affairs, both private and professional, and you have every intention of keeping it that way.

4 SATURDAY Woe betide those who keep holding you to impractical commitments. Your responsibility is to yourself, and if you feel like walking on the wild side, just get on with it; it's always nice to see a Bull breaking loose because generally speaking you're a creature of habit – but not right now.

5 SUNDAY You can always spot a fool when it comes to sussing out people's underlying motives, but someone's generosity

♉

is not what it seems to be. Right now, the stars are making you financially naïve. Therefore, make sure that you don't over-extend yourself, otherwise there could be a great deal of trouble looming in the near future.

6 MONDAY Just because you can do a million things at once, it doesn't mean you have to bend over backwards to do so for everybody else. It might be a good idea to let other people know that you're on a high and you don't intend to be deflated.

7 TUESDAY Don't kid yourself about how much you can, or are willing to, take on. By over-compensating for your sensitive side, you could come across as too self-assured and be snowed under. The stars are urging you to show off your talents, but resist. Quite honestly, you are better off maintaining a less desperate attitude; it's more admirable.

8 WEDNESDAY Venus is moving on into the fiery sign of Sagittarius and that's the area of your chart connected with shared resources, matters related to insurance and, to a degree, your relationships with others on the working front. If you need any favours then certainly this is the time to ask, so don't be too shy.

9 THURSDAY It's common knowledge that now is the time to make decisions about your future, whether you want to or not. However, there's no point in forcing yourself to hasty conclusions. Certain friends may think they know what's best for you, but ultimately it's your life. Lead it the way you want and don't back down because of pressure from others.

♉

10 FRIDAY For some time you have been having sleep-less nights or worried days because of certain people. Believe it or not, you are someone who requires space within your relationships. But you also prefer to know who loves you. Ask the right questions and you will hear the answers you want.

11 SATURDAY Achieving greater independence in your working life is important to you, but, although you are ready to bend the rules, you must be prepared to go along with the general consensus of opinion. If you have any misgivings about the venture you are embarking on, or your attitude to work, then you must stop and think very carefully.

12 SUNDAY There are certain areas in your life which need pruning to make way for beneficial change. Although you feel there is a sense of sparkle in the air concerning everything you do, it may be that you are simply glamorizing a new set of circumstances. Whatever the lure, don't give in to it. Instead, radiate happiness and you will succeed.

13 MONDAY The planets remind you that you are a secret romantic when the pressure of work or family demands are lifted, but you currently appear so involved in your personal challenges that there's little room for pleasure. Show someone close that you have a big warm heart. The only person who is giving you a hard time is yourself.

14 TUESDAY Loved ones are in the throes of great depths of feeling – always an emotional state you want to explore. However, they might not be willing to be your guinea pigs simply because they don't have your ability to review

♉

intimacy with such insight. Take care that you don't seem too analytical. Discover the truth with polite interest.

15 WEDNESDAY All that generosity is fine on the surface – which is why making an impulsive promise could be magical, but it is always regrettable. In the heat of the moment it might sound exciting and inspiring, but do you really believe you can live up to your commitment? Before you leap in, decide whether you want someone to get closer to your heart or not.

16 THURSDAY Certain people around you have very hungry egos, which means it's easier to take a back seat and let them get on with it. But, as your personal values are beginning to revolve around a new set of principles, you should assert yourself a little more than usual. If you make the effort it won't stop a clash of temperaments, but you will achieve much.

17 FRIDAY Today Mars will be moving into Sagittarius, the area of your chart devoted to club activities, friends, acquaintances and shared resources, and there might be a little bit of tension while this state of affairs exists. Luckily, you're the sort of person who can keep calm and that will be half the battle, so don't fret.

18 SATURDAY Today is the day of the Full Moon and it occurs in the water sign of Cancer. There's a warning here that you must take care when travelling from place to place. Neither is it a time to make any big move. If you do, you'll end up regretting it, and that would be a great pity.

19 SUNDAY Friends are making getting your message across interesting, as they are onlookers who would cause you to

♉

think one thing and say another. The best advice is that if you are fighting for a personal cause, speak from the heart. However, avoid appearing rebellious. It won't do you any favours when others are so conservative.

20 MONDAY Today the Sun will be moving into the airy sign of Aquarius and that, of course, is the zenith point of your chart - so from hereon in you are likely to be single minded where professional matters are concerned. Mind you, that is the way to go ahead, but make sure you don't tread on other people's toes. Remember – what goes around, comes around.

21 TUESDAY Something you believe to be a drain on your finances is proving to be an eye opener. In fact, you're realizing what your money means to you. The value you are placing on sorting things out means that you have the opportunity to make new commitments. Show others how capable you are when it comes to your own and their personal happiness.

22 WEDNESDAY The inspirational effects of the planets are giving you reason to feel positive. It seems as if your ambitious streak is about to shift up a gear. Move forward with confidence, and tell those less motivated friends that you won't shrink from a challenge. You owe it to yourself to prove you are adaptable. And that means others will support you too.

23 THURSDAY There are never any shortcuts or compromises where work is concerned. For once, bend the rules where certain colleagues are concerned – especially as you'll soon discover erratic, but highly capable, contributors are worth your

♉

time and consideration. Trust them, and you'll be pleasantly surprised. And, of course, relieved.

24 FRIDAY Someone else's past mistakes are usually the least of your worries, yet you're finding yourself becoming nothing more than a psychological go-between. Concern for others is fine, but not if it means you don't have the time to commit yourself where it really matters. Take it all with a pinch of salt and your obligations won't taste so one-sided.

25 SATURDAY Although a recent meeting with a persuasive individual means a lot, your natural tendency is to wait and see what happens. Hoping for miracles won't get you anywhere: you need a positive response, not a commitment. The planets' influence is making you indecisive, but at least let others know you're on their side.

26 SUNDAY Happily you are more open to the idea of pursuing an unconventional relationship than you thought you might be. And if you have been disenchanted with various other relationships, you'll realize that what they may have said is still of value. However, you need to move on. Now is the time to expand your associations and your network. Take this opportunity to make a foray into a different circle of people. The long-term benefits will be remarkable.

27 MONDAY Frankly, it's time to confront a rather delicate family situation. Think about the best way to deal with facts, especially as others have very little desire to pass comment or be realistic. What you are discovering is that happiness is not made – it is felt. Give others time, and very soon they will find this out too.

♉

28 TUESDAY The stars are activating your need to stay informed, but also to remain visibly neutral – particularly as over-heated opinions are freely flying between others. You have the courage to sort it all out, but however tempted you are to get involved, resist. You don't need an explosive situation to develop.

29 WEDNESDAY Your reputation and standing has been in doubt, but you are being urged to take command of a situation and show you mean business. Do so with audacity. Once in the swing of it, be careful you don't let it go to your head. Self-congratulation is fine, as long as you remember that not every pat on the back will be a genuine compliment.

30 THURSDAY In spite of the fact you'd rather not negotiate right now, you could achieve much by agreeing with every word spoken. Your tolerance level is admirable and, of course, you have no intention of causing a scene. However, a few niggling reservations are getting to you. Just don't give in to doubts and suspicions. You will achieve so much more.

31 FRIDAY Regardless of your need for a quieter existence, you can't stop others making certain demands. The planets' influences are urging you to negotiate even though you would rather turn your back and ignore it all. But it would be a mistake to be aloof when, for the sake of a little communication, you could make your life more tranquil.

FEBRUARY

The Sun this month is drifting through the airy sign of Aquarius up until the 18th. That's the area of your chart

♉

devoted to work, prestige, long-distance travel and foreigners, and in many ways it could be a novel and exciting time. Mind you, you could become obsessive about work and you need to keep a sense of proportion in that area. Furthermore, you may have a rather high opinion of yourself and if you start shouting your orders I'm afraid other people are not going to be impressed; you could lose some credibility.

On the 19th, the Sun will be moving into Pisces, the area of your chart devoted to friends, team effort and perhaps the redefining of your goals. It looks as if the stars are giving you a great deal to think about but, as a sensible Bull, you're sure to do the right thing by yourself and by other people too. Furthermore, late in the month, club activities and team effort are all emphasized, so it's going to be a happy-go-lucky period.

During this month, Mercury will be in Capricorn until the 12th, bringing minor changes and highlighting matters related to abroad and higher education, as well as team efforts and friends. At some point you may be asked to sign on the dotted line and, if so, do so with confidence.

On the 13th, Mercury moves into Aquarius, and so you may be asked to travel for the sake of work. Furthermore, you will be making contacts with people whom you will find useful at some point in the future, particularly if you find yourself in any kind of dilemma.

Venus will be in Sagittarius for the first four days of February, throwing a rosy glow over club activities, friendships and your social life generally. Once Venus moves on into Capricorn on the 5th, where it stays for the remainder of the month, your thoughts may stray to matters related to abroad and many of you may book a holiday, or perhaps there are people in your life who come from a different background to you, and this could be a learning period if that is the case.

♉

Mars will be situated in Sagittarius all month, the area of your chart devoted to team effort, professional contact and shared resources. Mind you, there may be a certain amount of tension in connection with these areas, but somebody's got to be sensible and as a Bull may I suggest that it be you?

The pattern made by the stars places strong emphasis on the signs of Aquarius and Capricorn and because of this you may be making an effort to improve your lot, not only for yourself but for your family and loved ones too. But then again, you are always a cherishing soul, aren't you Taurus?

1 SATURDAY Today is the day of the New Moon and it occurs in the airy sign of Aquarius. This indicates that there could be a fresh start or new opportunities at work, so take your blinkers off or otherwise they may pass you by. In fact, this is a great time for making any sort of fresh start.

2 SUNDAY This ought to be a time of pleasant encounters and developments, even though you may not know exactly what is going on in certain quarters. Indeed, others' motives or intentions are far more complex than you first thought. Nevertheless, you must be prepared to drop your guard and just accept situations for what they are.

3 MONDAY Today, there could be a change of plan – someone will explain everything to you once you get together. Perhaps you are on the brink of something extraordinary, having felt a bit empty recently – it seems that you have lost your contact with a kindred spirit. Now, however, your only problem is deciding which offer to accept when it comes to having fun.

♉

4 TUESDAY Those people who think they know all the answers will be surprised by your insight. It's not that you're trying to get one up on them, simply that you have had enough of listening to their boasting. The stars are making you feel that it might be a good idea to play a few mind games yourself, but don't bluff if you're put on the spot. This could only backfire at a later date.

5 WEDNESDAY Today Venus moves into Capricorn, the area of your chart devoted to travel and to friends who live abroad, and it's certain that you'll be hearing from one of your buddies around this time.

6 THURSDAY You don't want to seem awkward or uncompromising, but you have little choice when it comes to free advice. Someone else's demands are putting you to the test, and you know your own limits, especially regarding working affairs. Remember, you have the strength to resist such impositions on your time.

7 FRIDAY Being bogged down in so much work has been limiting your social life. Right now the stars are urging you to take time out for once and forget all about those responsibilities. Guilt doesn't have to replace your need to keep going. Simply remind others that you're entitled to a break as much as they are.

8 SATURDAY Financial problems aside, your ability to handle certain funds or expenditure is being challenged. Recognizing limitations to the material aspects of life is proving a problem, but you're not hampered by anyone other than

♉

yourself. Yes, it's hard to keep a track of it all, but with new insight you can improve your situation.

9 SUNDAY The Moon is making you want to say exactly what you feel, but the Sun is urging you to share the same sentiments as someone else, particularly regarding your joint resources. Of course, you have to be careful that you're in agreement. But somehow you're in the mood to be a little reckless. Take care you don't spoil a good arrangement.

10 MONDAY Making compromises is essential but you're assuming others know this too. The reality is that your sense of justice isn't the same as theirs. The planets are making you aware you should adopt a fairer view – it seems that it's up to you to show good faith when others are being difficult. Someone has to be generous, so why not you just for once?

11 TUESDAY Redefine your personal goals and let others attend to theirs. Strangely, you'll be much happier for it. You don't want to live on a cloud of confusion any more. Or do you? Your friends' and family beliefs seem to have muddled you. There are enough changes in your life to worry about without their uninvited asides. If they don't come round, then make sure at least you have their support. Choice words now mean genuine success in the near future.

12 WEDNESDAY Don't give up on something in your working life just because everyone seems to think you should. You have enough confidence now to pull it off, however wary you are about doing so. Quite likely you'll discover there is more

♉

joy in being true to your own principles than in following the crowd. Self-reliance will get you noticed.

13 THURSDAY Today Mercury will be moving into Aquarius, the zenith point of your chart, so there may be minor changes going on amongst members of your staff, or perhaps a change of direction is a possibility. However, your concentration is great and you're very focused. No one's going to steal a march on you, that's for sure.

14 FRIDAY There's a certain amount of tension in the stars at the moment, making you more aware of outstanding difficulties and differences of opinion. It's not that you want to fight, but you are feeling it's time to defend your views. That should ease the situation, but it might mean you come out feeling less than happy. It won't be easy, but you will have nothing to regret.

15 SATURDAY Someone out there is responding to your growing reputation. Frankly, you've been pushing harder than ever, and it is a time to set the records straight. However, you must remember that not everyone has your ability to be so succinct. Listen carefully to what is being said – your professional approach will be admired quicker than you imagined.

16 SUNDAY Look carefully at what is to be gained by upgrading your image, and what is to be lost by ignoring it. Whatever anyone says, you're working towards something reliable and worthwhile. The more you take care of Number 1 now, the more chances you have of long-term success. Your reputation is going to be enviable, so live up to it.

♉

17 MONDAY Spare a moment for your personal involvements. You are seeing clearly how to role-play when required, but that doesn't mean you are always true to yourself. By all means act the part that others anticipate, but remember that you're just doing what's right for now. It will be much more interesting when you take time out to be yourself.

18 TUESDAY There's always something inspiring about a challenge, particularly when it concerns your ambitions. Undoubtedly, you do have your reasons for coercing others and you're beginning to realize that you can make all kinds of waves when you want to. However, extend your thinking to more liberal ideas – others will love you for it.

19 WEDNESDAY Today the Sun will be moving into Pisces, the area of your chart devoted to friends, acquaintances, redefining your goals and your imagination, which is firing on all cylinders. Should you have a Piscean in your life, then you can be quite sure that you'll get plenty of back-up from them over the next couple of weeks or so.

20 THURSDAY Although you are practical about managing your worries on your own, it seems a friendly ear would be more than welcome for a change. You don't usually feel the need to download your troubles on anybody else, but a timely chat with someone close means you can be much more charitable with yourself. You have the right to do that once in a while.

21 FRIDAY The planets have certainly got you hooked on making dazzling impressions. Yet others are still whingeing about why you have to be so self-centred. Quite honestly they don't have a leg to stand on, especially as you know you won't let them down. But you do have to think of your own needs too. Remember to be true to yourself first.

22 SATURDAY Remain enthusiastic and affable when a loved one becomes elusive. You're far more likely to draw their interest by being your usual exuberant self. Any attempt to change the atmosphere will only make them act more like a fugitive. It's not your fault if they're feeling unsettled. Genuine affection will help, but trusting in your nerve is better.

23 SUNDAY Inhibitions about divulging personal needs are slowly being lifted. You must ask yourself whether it's better to keep your private thoughts under lock and key, or let others know the truth. Yes, it might be easier just to close up shop and go home, but rather than pretending it doesn't matter, revealing all will mean you can sleep more soundly.

24 MONDAY Your reputation is about to soar. You're feeling ready to take control of any situation, and you should do so with your usual tenacity. But remember, once you get into the swing of things, you might not know when to stop. Others aren't responsible for your achievements, but they might help you slow down a bit.

25 TUESDAY You desperately need information before you'll agree to certain rules, but all that you seem to be getting is aggravation. In fact, because you seem so worryingly sharp, it's hardly surprising that others feel insecure. With the planets' help you'll begin to get the kind of data you want. Adapt, rather than resist, and you'll find exactly what you're seeking.

♉

26 WEDNESDAY A clash in the stars is stopping you from making yourself understood. But you can't be blamed for sticking to certain rules when others are apparently being difficult. Your courage won't fail you, so, if they are seeking ultimatums, make them wait. Trust in your perception and enjoy all that's about to unfold.

27 THURSDAY Privately you are set on a change of priorities. And a calculated risk won't bring any problems, as long as you have the integrity to back it up – especially as others seem to have a more pessimistic attitude. If they have good reason for doubting you, then fine. But if they're neurotic because of their own insecurities, you're better off going it alone.

28 FRIDAY Pressure from others about developing your ideas is giving you yet another angle on life. And you're beginning to get quite excited. The planets are urging you to make an impression before somebody else does. When you are in one of your reforming moods, there's nothing really to hold you back – except perhaps self-doubt.

MARCH

This month the Sun will be drifting through Pisces until the 20th. That's the area of your chart devoted to friends, team efforts, socializing and generally letting your troubles drift away and enjoying yourself. If you've a Pisces in your life, and you need some kind of advice, that is the sign to go to and they'll willingly help you out.

♉

On the 21st, the Sun will be moving into Aries, increasing your imagination, your instincts and your ability to know what needs to be done at the right time. Don't let anybody else sway you: you know what you're doing even if they don't think so.

Mercury will be in Aquarius for the first four days of the month, so you still have a little time for making minor changes at work if you deem it necessary. Once Mercury moves into Pisces on the 5th, it will be an excellent time for attending to paperwork and travelling.

Mercury moves on again on the 22nd, this time into Aries; this is the secretive area of your chart, but it will certainly be stimulating for your imagination and your instincts, and the only question is, are you going to listen? I sincerely hope so. Should you have an Aries in your life, they'll be a little bit changeable and difficult to handle, but fortunately you've plenty of patience.

Venus will be in Capricorn for the first couple of days and if you have somebody in your life born under this sign, that will be a good person to go to for advice or maybe simply for having a good time.

On 3 March, Venus moves into Aquarius, the zenith point of your chart, and this will certainly bode well if you have creative ambitions, or if you want to form a professional partnership. Push ahead and don't let anybody dissuade you. This advice holds good up until the 27th.

Mars will be coasting along in Sagittarius for the first few days, so if you are part of a team you can expect a certain amount of tension and hard work, but you're not afraid of that now, are you?

On the 5th, Mars will be moving into the earthy sign of Capricorn, and so you may be getting a little bit tense because you're unsure exactly what direction you should be heading for. Relax and be kind to yourself for a short while, and everything will become abundantly clear.

The pattern made by the stars this month places the emphasis in the sign of Pisces, so if you have someone important in your life born under this sign, it would be a good idea to go to them for advice if necessary. Or should you be worried, they'll be able to put your mind at ease. I have to say that it's not often that a Bull admits that's he's in a bit of a 'lather', but you are only human, Taurus, so take that on board.

1 SATURDAY The Moon right now is in the airy sign of Aquarius, the zenith point of your chart, so if you want to make any minor changes where work matters are concerned, now is the time for getting cracking in this direction.

2 SUNDAY Someone isn't quite all they seem. In fact, what you've been imagining and what is reality are two different things. Due to the tension in the stars, a loved one has been acting strangely, but put it down to a bout of egotism rather than anything personal. Now you can begin to understand not only the whys and wherefores of a close liaison, but also how you can improve your life. You're not alone, and it takes two to make a relationship work, remember that.

3 MONDAY Today is the day of the New Moon and it occurs in the water sign of Pisces, the area of your chart devoted to the redefining of goals, club activities, casual acquaintances and, of course, close friends. So now you know where to go if you have any doubts.

4 TUESDAY Trying to find a happy medium between what you know to be the truth and what is purely a hunch is understandably difficult. The stars are making you doubt your own intuitions. It may leave you feeling slightly uneasy, but you have more reason to feel happy about your pragmatic streak. Work with it and you'll find it to be of benefit.

5 WEDNESDAY The starry set-up today is now superb. You should be in excellent spirits and will also be able to recharge your batteries, which you probably desperately need to do! But certain people are bound to turn up without warning. While you ought to react with glee, you maybe somewhat puzzled as to their motives.

6 THURSDAY Mercury is now in Pisces, the area of your chart devoted to team effort, the defining of goals, friends and acquaintances. It looks as if you're in for a pretty sociable time over the next few days, so let your hair down and enjoy yourself.

7 FRIDAY The stars are bringing out the softer and more diplomatic side to your character. It will be a less aggressive day for those who are involved in a partnership or in connection with the arts. If this applies to you, push ahead with any plans you may have, as you've precious little to lose.

8 SATURDAY Although there is some good news on a family or business matter, you may not be that keen when it comes to putting up the money. You certainly wouldn't want to go behind somebody else's back if you can smooth things over with them. Either way, by the end of this day, there's likely to be some fun and games.

ȣ

9 SUNDAY Don't go completely wild if a close partner or friend says exactly the opposite of what you were expecting. They may just be trying to wind you up. You cannot decide whether to cling on possessively at the moment, or fight for freedom. However, getting into power struggles with friends or even lovers is hardly constructive; just live and let live.

10 MONDAY It seems that you have come to the point in your life where you're willing to put up with just so much and no more. Where loved ones or the family are concerned, you are clear now that you intend to protect your own needs and will not be pulled by old duties that are no longer relevant to you. Give yourself a few hours this evening in order to wind down – you're most certainly going to need it.

11 TUESDAY Due to some splendid planetary aspects there are likely to be some heart-warming responses or experiences. There again, others will try to tell you that they are unhappy in themselves, but you may need to read between the lines. In the circumstances, it would probably be best not to provoke them for the time being.

12 WEDNESDAY There may be some good news where cash matters are concerned. However, you must guard against the inclination to turn into a spendthrift. If you cave in, it's going to be an extremely expensive day and one you will regret for some while to come.

13 THURSDAY Again you must take note of what partners and other people tell you. This should be a time of amazing revelations, even if you're not sure what you intend to do. This is particularly true if you have flaunted one relationship

♉

and can now imagine how hurt someone was by this. Perhaps you don't want to know.

14 FRIDAY Over the past few days you have been strangely silent because you believed no one was listening to your ideas. Now this will all change, but your mind will be leaping from subject to subject at lightning speed. You will need to slow down for those confused companions who are still operating at the normal rate. Not all of your plans can be put into action instantly, but you are certainly on the starting blocks.

15 SATURDAY Though the stars may not bring any visible change to your way of behaving, it's likely that you are far more sensible, grounded and practical than is usually the case. You are provided with a wonderful day, then, for making important decisions.

16 SUNDAY Today you'll be getting your own way. You've plenty of confidence, loads of charm, and it shouldn't be difficult to achieve whatever you desire. Right now, the emphasis could be on money and saving. So it's lucky that you have at least a few days at this time for putting matters straight.

17 MONDAY Today you may have to travel for the sake of money, whilst others may be signing important documents. Either way, things will be lucky for you, so it's a time for pushing ahead.

18 TUESDAY This is the day of the Full Moon and it occurs in the earthy sign of Virgo – the area of your chart devoted to casual romance, creativity and matters related to children. But it has to be said that there could be complications in these areas so don't take anything for granted – you'll regret it. This is a good time for putting the finishing touches to work and projects.

19 WEDNESDAY You're in that frame of mind when you'll be drawn to those who are perhaps 'out of bounds'. In other words, people who already have someone significant in tow. This is unlike you, because as a rule you are an honest and truthful person. Maybe the sexual attraction is so strong that it cannot be resisted, but if you take my advice, you'll do your best to do just that. Otherwise you'll be storing up hurt in the coming weeks.

20 THURSDAY The stars are making you impulsive and greedy. Luckily, this state of affairs won't last too long so you should be able to cope without getting yourself into any kind of 'strife' or trouble. See what you can do.

21 FRIDAY Today the Sun will be moving into the fiery sign of Aries, so there's an awful lot going on in the background and it's up to you to make sure that you know exactly where you stand and what's happening. Should you have an Aries in your life then they're going to be full of confidence and will be an ideal person to go to for advice, or simply 'moral support'.

22 SATURDAY Why be timid when you can take on a much higher profile? If you feel particularly lacking in confidence at the moment, you can always put on an act. Fake a grand gesture, or at least push to make sure someone understands that you intend to be seen, heard and applauded during the coming days. You're more in demand than you realize, both socially and at work.

23 SUNDAY You can expect those who are closest to you, both at work and at home, to be changeable and maybe, if you are unlucky, obstructive. This then is clearly a day to brush off your independence and put it to good use.

24 MONDAY There's likely to be some good news on the financial level. Furthermore, many of you may decide to take a new relationship much more seriously than you had intended, but please don't panic if this should be the case. Bide your time and see how matters develop over the coming days before you make a decision.

25 TUESDAY If you can content yourself with keeping an ear close to the ground and listening to the whispers on the wind, it will benefit you greatly in the near future. If you insist on standing on your soapbox, megaphone in hand, you may find you get a blank response. Just recognize that letting others take centre-stage for a few days, or even a couple of weeks, could be a wise move.

26 WEDNESDAY If you've been waiting to hear from friends or relatives abroad, then you shouldn't be disappointed today. However, if this doesn't occur, then it is still an ideal time for any kind of team effort and making minor changes in your life, but nothing too major.

27 THURSDAY Today you're full of confidence and good humour, and you are a positive delight to spend time with. Furthermore, you will find that other people are willing to help you out in any way they can, if only you ask. Someone new who enters your life is likely to be important for a while.

ৰ

28 FRIDAY Today Venus moves into Pisces, the area of your chart devoted to friends and acquaintances, and it's an extremely sociable time. So let your hair down, without spending too much money, and you'll be able to let go of some negative feelings that have been troubling you.

29 SATURDAY Never one to concentrate on detail when you can off-load boring practical chores onto somebody else's shoulders, you're now facing a fairly self-disciplined day whether you like it or not. So you will have to apply yourself to streamlining your activities, cutting out waste, and seeing what you can do to get fit. If you are in fighting form, you will slide easily through everyday tasks.

30 SUNDAY Younger friends and team mates are the ones to keep you on your toes and will challenge you to adopt pioneering plans. This is no time to be a stick-in-the-mud. Instead, you should be looking ahead with vibrant confidence. Picking the right company to travel alongside is one sure way of keeping your enthusiasm high.

31 MONDAY Luckily, your sense of humour is at last beginning to bounce back. Whatever has happened is now water under the bridge and you can sense that your popularity is beginning to rise. Talk to loved ones, friends and children. They will appreciate your jokes and make you glow in the spotlight at odd moments. You will also turn a disaster into a major triumph.

♉

APRIL

During April, the Sun will be coasting along in the fiery sign of Aries up until the 20th. That's a part of your chart that rules instincts, matters behind the scenes and maybe even your sub-conscious. It will be a good idea, then, to 'feel' your way through life at this time because you could pick up on opportunities and ideas while doing so.

Once the Sun moves into Taurus on the 21st, you begin your 'solar' part of the year: a time when you can make life stand on its head and see things from your point of view. For heaven's sake don't waste this. All too often we have to 'kowtow' to other people's wants and demands, but this time, for you, you are something of a free agent, so make the most of it.

Mercury will be in Aries up until 5 April, so you've lots of good ideas and your imagination takes flight. If you're in a creative job you'll certainly be doing very well. On the 6th, Mercury will be moving into your own sign of Taurus, so it's possible that you may be asked to travel for the sake of your job, or mix with foreigners. Either, or both, will be a good idea.

However, Mercury will go into retrograde movement on the 26th, so from hereon in, until this situation rectifies itself, it wouldn't be a good idea to go in for unnecessary travelling, or signing paperwork without the advice of a solicitor. It may cost you a few pennies, but, believe you me, you'll save yourself an awful lot of trouble in the long run.

Venus will be situated in Pisces up until 21 April, the area of your chart devoted to friends, shared resources and team efforts. Put your shoulder to the wheel in these areas because you won't regret it. On the 22nd, Venus moves into Aries. Oh dear! There is a suggestion here that you may not be up-front

♉

where your love life is concerned. Maybe you'll discover that magnetic sexual attraction; if you've got a partner at home may I suggest that you forget about this, because not to do so could really land you in hot water.

Mars also remains in Capricorn until the 21st – the area of your chart devoted to travelling or legal matters, which could provide a source of strain and stress. Getting in one or two early nights will help matters considerably; then you won't get things out of proportion.

On the 22nd, Mars moves into Aquarius where it stays for the remainder of the month. A hard-working time and one that will benefit you in the future, so keep at it; believe you me, you're not wasting your time.

The pattern made by the stars suggests that you are in control of your fate, both for good and bad, so have the confidence of your convictions and you'll find that other people will be willing to help you achieve them – providing, of course, you use a certain amount of charm. Certainly it will be a hard-working period, but you might receive some help from somebody born under a fire sign. Snap it up – you won't regret it, I can assure you.

1 TUESDAY Today is the day of the New Moon and it occurs in the fiery sign of Aries. Your instincts and perceptions are unbeatable right now, so make the most of them both at work and also in your personal life. If you do this others will be quite surprised at your insight and you are bound to gain in the long run.

2 WEDNESDAY Over the next couple of days there'll be times when you could be completely reckless, spending more than you can earn and may finish up in debt. On the other hand, if

♉

you use a spot of enterprise and enthusiasm you can gain, but watch out for those gigantic pitfalls.

3 THURSDAY They always say that ruts in a road flatten out if you drive fast enough. No one is suggesting you should take too many risks, but there's no doubt that you are moving in the right direction at the moment, where work and your reputation are concerned. All the right people will be impressed by your wit, wisdom and inspired ideas, so spread yourself around as much as you can manage.

4 FRIDAY Don't be surprised if work which is at all artistic or creative is blocked in some way. Some of you may find that your social life is changing at the last minute and this will make you feel a little bit disconcerted and even grumpy. But believe you me, this is because the lives of other people are out of control for the time being.

5 SATURDAY Not all the confidential discussions are out of the way yet, but you are certainly feeling a little breath of fresh air at the moment. You feel positively enlivened by nature now, and rather keen to take off on your own and not worry too much about all those tedious chores. Whatever new agreements are in place at the moment will just have to do as far as you are concerned – for now anyway.

6 SUNDAY Today Mercury will be moving into Taurus and that's the area of your chart devoted to money, resources and possessions. There could be some problems with these sides to life, but they'll only be minor and there is really nothing for you to worry about. On the other hand, if you're signing any kind of contract, you couldn't have a better day!

♉

7 MONDAY Do you believe your everyday routine will speed up even more now? You probably hope not, because you feel dizzy enough trying to cope with the millions of details as it is. You know perfectly well that you are secretly pleased with having absolutely no room for boredom. There are letters to write, phone calls to make and heaps of people to visit. It may be more quantity than quality, but you are covering a lot of territory.

8 TUESDAY The day ahead will be a chatty, highly strung and not always cooperative one, but you are forging a new path for yourself and trying out new things at work. Money will improve in some way, and so should your sex life.

9 WEDNESDAY All of your more positive qualities are on display. You become more loving, thoughtful and caring. The humanitarian within is only too willing to reach out to other people. You can be quite sure that what you do over the next few weeks will be well received by other people.

10 THURSDAY Right now you could turn into something of a skinflint, holding onto your cash and being very reluctant to part with any of it. Mind you, if you happen to work in banking or the financial professions, you should be doing exceptionally well.

11 FRIDAY It wouldn't be a good idea to travel too far, neglect your method of transport or sign any kind of paperwork which commits you to long-term payments. Be alert, too, to minor mistakes that you and other people could make. A little bit of thought will take you a long way.

♉

12 SATURDAY With any luck, money that is owed will come rolling in. Furthermore, you'll be in a mood for spending in order to enjoy yourself, or perhaps to please other people. Either way, it looks as if it's going to be a rather charming day.

13 SUNDAY If you feel you're up against one tricky situation too many right now, then sometimes a tactical retreat is the best way of handling the tangle. Step into the background until you have a clearer idea of how you can get your own way. There'll be confidential agreements to be re-negotiated, whether emotional or financial, in the coming days and you will want to investigate these thoroughly so you can come to the fairest terms.

14 MONDAY After a hectic couple of days there's a need to wind down. Everything should even out a good deal now. The stars are cheering where one relationship is concerned. But you need to rouse yourself, get a grip and make the most of a chance to straighten things out. Love and compliments could start to wing their way in your direction, so climb off the shelf and back into the spotlight.

15 TUESDAY At times you need to find a better way of balancing your needs for independence with the needs of close partners. Clearly, you need support and reassurance from those who are very important so that you have enough elbow room to steer your own course. The affectionate compliments of someone special will make your way a good deal smoother from now on.

16 WEDNESDAY Today is the day of the Full Moon and it happens in the airy sign of Libra. Oh dear! There could be

♉

quarrels and disagreements on the work front today. Try to remember that other people can also have good ideas – and they may even occasionally be better than your own! If you keep this in mind you are likely to prevent any bad feelings.

17 THURSDAY It's quite likely you will dig up a strong attraction for someone. If you happen to have a partner in tow you need to be extremely careful, because it's likely that this attraction is purely sexual and you mustn't endanger a relationship that holds a great deal more for you.

18 FRIDAY If family matters are hanging rather heavily on your mind, don't worry too much. You might just be over-reacting to a slightly tangled situation. Put regrets firmly behind you, and decide to make the best of a rather routine day that lies ahead. You may not be inclined for adventure, but there will be highlights and fun moments at work, and relationships improve too.

19 SATURDAY Today you could be rather impatient and unaccommodating. Heaven help anyone who tries to ask for a favour from you on this particular day, as they're likely to get their head bitten off. Do try to be a little kinder to those who mean the most to you.

20 SUNDAY If you feel you are travelling away from things which seem to be offering you love and security, then be reassured. This is only a temporary blip and will give you the time you need to re-assess what is really valuable. More than anything you need a chance to step back and reflect. There may be fewer social invitations for a couple of days but this can be a blessing in disguise. Be philosophical.

♉

21 MONDAY Today the Sun will be moving into the earthy sign of Taurus, which is, of course, your sign. Therefore, you'll look good, feel good and have much more confidence over the next couple of weeks or so – so make the most of it.

22 TUESDAY Today Venus will be moving into Aries which could be a little bit 'dodgy'. If you're not getting on well with your partner, then you may be tempted to stray, even though it goes against the grain; do control yourself though.

23 WEDNESDAY The day ahead will be special, with decisions that will prove beneficial to relationships and work. Money will flow in faster and with less effort than expected. But rest and exercise is, I'm afraid, needed – so take heed.

24 THURSDAY Whatever emotional upsets there have been, they are now behind you, so you ought to be heading towards better times. Any minor setbacks should not prove a major hassle with your determination. Keep in mind that looking forward is crucial. Remaining stuck on the spot, or regretting the past, is a waste of time and energy.

25 FRIDAY The urge to get away from it all proves difficult to resist today. You may have far to go and have much to organize, so you'd better start early and avoid being caught in a rush. Recent events should have made it abundantly clear that you have to free yourself from those who tend to restrict or restrain you.

26 SATURDAY You'll find it difficult to sit still for too long. Indeed, it's a good time for keeping on the go, making contact with other people and maybe asking for a few favours. If you're single, get out this evening and make sure that you are highly visible, because a new romance is a distinct possibility.

27 SUNDAY There's certainly a lively feel about this 24-hour period. The males in your circle will be extremely helpful and anxious about your welfare, but anything that crops up unexpectedly should be dissected and analysed before you reject it.

28 MONDAY There's a happy glow over short-distance travelling and your relationships with neighbours and acquaintances. It may be that a brother or sister is in need of some advice or attention, and if that should be the case you will certainly not be letting them down.

29 TUESDAY There should be a reason to splash out now, even if others don't approve or try to put you on the spot. They are probably wondering if there's anything in it for them. The question is whether you'll be able to do your own thing without being caught out – you'll never know unless you try.

30 WEDNESDAY Although you must be prepared for some awkward moments now, try not to get carried away. Admittedly, you may have been a bit indiscreet of late, but you should now realize that others have problems that they couldn't explain. In fact, what you discover now ought to bring about a reconciliation.

MAY

The Sun this month will be coasting along in your own sign of Taurus until the 20th, and you begin your time of the year when you will be looking great, and will be ready to take on anybody who stands in your way. Try not to be too ruthless, though, as this could backfire on you.

On the 21st, the Sun will be entering Gemini – the area of your chart devoted to money and cash. Because of this you'll be far more inclined to save rather than spend, and although this may not go down well with loved ones, you're basically looking after their best interests. If only they would understand that!

Mercury continues its retrograde action in your sign until the 20th, when it finally sees sense. So don't sign any important paperwork or travel unnecessarily at this time, otherwise you'll run into problem after problem.

Venus will be in Aries until 15 May. That's a secretive area of your chart so your instincts are firing on all cylinders, and if you are at all creative you'll do exceptionally well.

Once Venus enters your own sign on the 16th, you really can't go wrong. Relationships, work and everything in life seems to be given the green light from the stars, so do make the most of this period because, let's face it, it doesn't last that long.

Mars continues its journey through Aquarius all month. This is the zenith point of your chart and is usually connected with work where, I'm afraid, you're going to be toiling a great deal harder than is usually the case. Maybe there are snags or hold-ups that are causing this state of affairs, but either way you'll just have to put your shoulder to the wheel and put up with it. If a Bull can't survive little trials and tribulations then, I'm afraid, nobody else can, so take heart.

♉

The pattern made by the stars suggests that you throw away some of your old ideas and take on board that which is new. Furthermore, new people will be entering your life, giving you a fresh slant on some worn out ideas. Don't be too proud to admit that perhaps you might be just a touch wrong; if you can do that, you'll be making progress in life and that, after all, is the idea. Nobody wants to be marching on the same spot forever now, do they? Certainly not you.

1 THURSDAY Well, May certainly gets off to a good start, mainly because there's a beautiful New Moon and, guess what, it's in your sign. What better omen could you have than that. Confidence will be swelling and anyone who thinks they can order you around or take advantage of you is in for a big surprise.

2 FRIDAY Today money that is owed can be cheerfully chased and you can afford to splash out on minor purchases. But just make sure that you don't take this to extremes, otherwise you may find yourself in trouble later.

3 SATURDAY By all accounts the time has come to follow the dictates of your heart. Meanwhile, others are bound to try to influence your choices or decisions, which may reinforce the isolation you feel. In any event, this day marks a major turning point and you must take responsibility for your actions.

4 SUNDAY The stars seem to be hinting that over the next couple of days or so there'll be a great deal of movement. You should meet interesting new people while travelling from place to place. Therefore keep your ears and eyes wide open, because there's a chance of romance.

♉

5 MONDAY There's a stop/go feel about this particular day, which may be frustrating in at least one particular area. However, when dealing with people who are considerably older than you, you may find them far more open-minded and ready for action than you could possibly have believed.

6 TUESDAY The stars are doing wonders for your morale right now. Whatever the ups and downs, you know there are supportive companions around. They may not be entirely realistic at times, but at least they are reassuring. Be more protective of your secrets later today, because you need to work out in your mind what you hope to gain. Don't be subtle: pull a few strings and see your hopes materialize.

7 WEDNESDAY It seems that the penny has finally dropped and you are beginning to discover there is a different way of living and perhaps loving. For such a long time you have been ploughing one furrow; now you know it is within your power to move to a different sphere of influence. Don't worry, close partners may be surprised but they will eventually adapt, although it may take some time.

8 THURSDAY A less than satisfactory situation at home or at work can no longer be allowed to continue, and you must consider making serious moves to end it. Positive starry influences are giving you the opportunity to enhance your future by cutting links that are locking you into the past. The fact is that you already know in your heart what has to be done – it's just a case of convincing your head.

9 FRIDAY Your confidence today means that you can create high positive results with less effort than usual. You should

♉

just keep looking enthusiastically in the right direction. At least a fraction of your dreams are coming true at last. If you are not entirely satisfied with the state of your close relationships, then push harder and demand more. The tide seems to be turning your way, romantically speaking.

10 SATURDAY The stars seem to be emphasizing the family and some happy news seems to be winging its way in your direction. Those of you who have a contract that is coming to an end should leap into action and make a serious effort to renew it.

11 SUNDAY Pushing on with chores in an understated, low key way is probably wise. You need a chance every so often to sit back and recharge your batteries, so leaping into ambitious projects would not be wise right now. Close partners may be less than positive when you unfold some of your ideas. But you have a persuasive tongue in your head, so they should come round to your way of thinking.

12 MONDAY You may not be in the mood to consider whether what you are doing is a sensible use of your time, energy or ideas, but if you don't conduct just such a review now, you are in danger of getting things wrong when opportunities arise and your resources could be seriously overstretched, which would be a pity.

13 TUESDAY A flirtation at work can keep you happily occupied for a couple of weeks. It may be that you feel rather self-sacrificing where loved ones are concerned, giving more than you are getting. You need a few moments of relaxation

♉

and entertainment somewhere. If you have a chance to sort out better rules and regulations for the future where the family is concerned, it will be to everybody's benefit.

14 WEDNESDAY If you feel fearful of getting the thumbs down from one of your schemes, then maybe you need to ask where you lie, or whether you are just being slightly neurotic. Take a good look to get things in perspective. Stand back and try to see other people's points of view for a change. Maybe their intentions are not what you think.

15 THURSDAY The planets are giving you greater confidence when it comes to sorting out cash problems. If ever there was a day for visits to the bank manager, then this is it, because he/she is likely to be open-minded and receptive.

16 FRIDAY Today is the day of the Full Moon and it occurs in your opposite sign of Scorpio, so there's no point in expecting cooperation, or even any thought from other people. Just go it alone – you're good at that – and try not to hold any kind of grudge, as that would be fruitless.

17 SATURDAY Venus has now moved into your own sign, which is good news because you're going to be looking good, feeling good and will have far more confidence than is usually the case. So make the next couple of weeks work for you, won't you?

18 SUNDAY It is unlike you to allow other people's lack of enthusiasm to keep you from taking some sort of action, but with the current planetary set-up you must play a waiting game. Soon it will be over and then their attitude will be set to

♉

change. Only after this can discretion bear any kind of fruit, as to try to take action before this would be a waste of time.

19 MONDAY It is rare for you to have a change of heart once you've committed yourself to something and, whether the situation is personal or professional, you believe loyalty is always a priority. Don't let this mean, however, that you avoid facing potentially unpleasant but vital facts about certain individuals or situations.

20 TUESDAY Today Mercury resumes direct movement so you need not fear paperwork, travelling or people younger than yourself. You can push ahead with renewed confidence, which should put you in good stead. If you have Geminis or Virgos in your life they are likely to be the ones who are sure to make your evening happy and fun.

21 WEDNESDAY Today the Sun will be moving into the airy sign of Gemini and that's the area of your chart devoted to money and possessions. You're doing quite well in these areas. If you decide to go bargain hunting you'll pick up something quite valuable and will be pleased with yourself for quite some time to come.

22 THURSDAY With so much happening it's not surprising that you feel overwrought: even situations that seemed set in stone could change. When it comes to matters involving your work or reputation, you really cannot afford to be seen to compromise, much less give the impression that you don't care.

23 FRIDAY If you're confronted by tension and conflict today, then it is important that you rise above it and concentrate all

♉

of your energies into what you have in common with work-mates and others. Do keep looking to the future with your unique brand of optimism and flexibility. It is likely to be a rewarding as well as a learning time, especially when you have been able to solve an emotional problem that may have been troubling you.

24 SATURDAY If you happen to work in a creative job you'll certainly be doing well and receiving lots of praise. Do make sure, though, that this doesn't go to your head, otherwise it may deflect you from carrying on in the successful way you have been.

25 SUNDAY Itchy feet may get you into trouble, if you let it be known that you want to be somewhere else, or with some-one else. You have the right to feel aggrieved if your move-ments are restricted and you cannot go where you want to. If you leave now, you'll be conspicuous by your absence.

26 MONDAY Someone in authority may see how best to use your talents. Without being confrontational, outline your ideas in plain simple language. From where you're standing you can see that opportunities are being wasted and money might even be lost. You have been quiet for too long. Start making a noise.

27 TUESDAY At best you appear active and purposeful. At worst, stubborn and nervous. Make sure with today's plane-tary set-up you harness your energies. One inspired idea will trigger off the next. Just make sure you don't suffer from burnout or run yourself into the ground.

♉

28 WEDNESDAY Invitations are likely to arrive from all directions, but before accepting any of them you must sit down and work out which will offer the most in the way of enjoyment, and perhaps romance. A little bit of thought will take you a long way on this day.

29 THURSDAY You're wondering why others are so keen to have you in their midst and to see you enjoying yourself. You have struck the right chord with friends or associates, who are becoming more impressed with you as time goes on. Rest assured that any explanation needed will arrive when the time is right.

30 FRIDAY You can't expect to be happy if you're involved in routine or mundane jobs when you are so hungry for innovation and inspiration. It must be as plain as day that your agile mind is under-employed and your abilities are going to waste. If this needs spelling out to those in positions of power, do it now.

31 SATURDAY You may have been putting off discussions about the practical side of domestic arrangements because you find them unexciting, but now they are demanding to be tackled. Do it now and not only will you get them out of the way, but those whose attitude most worried you will be interested, if not helpful.

JUNE

The Sun this month will be drifting through the airy sign of Gemini up until the 21st and that's the area of your chart devoted to money – not that you'll be getting so much in, but

♉

you are definitely in a frame of mind for saving. Perhaps you've got an item, or maybe a holiday, in view and that is what is stimulating you. Besides, one person in your family has got to be sensible, haven't they?

On the 22nd, the Sun will be moving into Cancer, the area of your chart devoted to the mind, which is likely to be quite ingenious. Furthermore, any travelling you do for the sake of business will certainly be well rewarded. Should you have a brother or sister, they're going to be playing a prominent role in your affairs at this time. Whether you like it or not, though, is something else.

Mercury will be in Taurus until 12 June and this, of course, is your sign. You're much more flexible and approachable at this time. Others may wonder what's come over you, but don't knock it – enjoy it. On the 13th, Mercury will move into Gemini where, of course, it finds the Sun for a little while until the 29th, when it courses off into watery Cancer. Again the emphasis is on saving and money in general; there may even be enough for you to put it away for a rainy day – how very nice.

Venus remains in your own sign until the 9th, but no one can complain about that because this always has a positive influence – unless, of course, you're going to over-indulge in food or drink, which is a weakness of the Bull. But maybe that doesn't apply to you, just to others.

Venus moves into Gemini on the 10th, where it stays till the end of the month. Once more, then, you seem to be raking in money that's owed but, of course, you will spend occasionally. You're not likely to go over the top as, for example, a Sagittarius would.

Mars coasts along in Aquarius until 16 June, when you can expect to work hard for your cash. Nothing's going to come

♉

easy, but luckily you are a patient soul and should be able to survive. On the 17th, Mars will be entering Pisces and the area of your chart devoted to team effort, club activities and friendships. Mind you, there could be some moments of tension here if you insist on bulldozing in, trying to boss everybody around – that's not the way to go. Put on the charm, as usual, and you won't go wrong.

The pattern made by the stars places considerable emphasis on matters related to abroad or higher education. It could be that you have decided to learn a new skill and, if so, you have picked a good time for doing so and, of course, as a Bull you will see it through to the bitter end, even if eventually you decide that it is not a skill you want to develop in any way, shape or form!

1 SUNDAY Sometimes life can seem hard and full of difficulties and you may feel discouraged, but in the long run there is little that you have to face that is too challenging or that you can't find a solution to. Even so, just remember that thinking things through can take time, but the end result will probably be all the better for it.

2 MONDAY There seems to be a lighthearted feel to your social life and, regardless of your own sex, it is likely that female friends will be more important than anyone else. They will be handing on useful information and perhaps making exciting introductions too, which will help to overcrowd your social calendar – which is just the way you like it.

3 TUESDAY It seems that the older and more experienced members of your circle are likely to be getting in touch with you. They may need some sort of emotional support for a little while and should this be the case, you'll be your usual friendly self and supply it.

4 WEDNESDAY No matter how contented you are to be tied with your home and family, your enquiring mind may lead you further afield, possibly even to foreign shores. Previous attempts at exploring something similar may have been thwarted. Now you are older and wiser and should tell yourself failure is simply not an option.

5 THURSDAY If you're tempted to probe into another person's problems, you are not dealing in idle gossip, but do have a genuine desire to help. You, more than most, appreciate the true worth of loyal and trusted confidences. Have no doubt in your ability to strengthen ties weakened by events of the past few days.

6 FRIDAY Something comes to light to make you wonder about the integrity of a colleague or a companion who has always had your trust and respect. Try not to be too critical until all the facts come to light. You might be basing your judgement on unreliable information, and there is no room for error.

7 SATURDAY You have every right to indulge in an unusual form of entertainment, but, whereas others happily stretch their budget on such occasions, you might not be willing to pay the price of something you know little about. If you decide to give it a miss, don't complain later about being hard up or hard done by.

♉

8 SUNDAY Although you appear to go along with what others want you to believe, deep down you know something is amiss. The astrological set-up today will bring to the surface the cause of your concern. It will then be up to you to decide at what point to raise the alarm. Precise timing could mean you win the battle hands down.

9 MONDAY It is some measure of your success that you have more competitors than ever. But don't feel nervous of your position. Just tell yourself you deserve whatever acclaim comes your way. In both your personal and your professional life you have hidden strengths others cannot rival.

10 TUESDAY Today Venus will be moving into Gemini and the area of your chart devoted to cash matters and your earning power, which is going to be quite considerable over the next few days, or even few weeks. However, do make sure that you don't spend as quickly as you gain – that would be foolhardy.

11 WEDNESDAY The stars are filling you with confidence, goodwill and making you extremely attractive to other people. It's difficult to imagine that you will not have made at least one new contact before this day is over, and in some cases this could lead to serious romance.

12 THURSDAY Even if someone is being mean, there's no point in causing a huge furore. People tend to do what they want and you must sometimes stand back and let them make their own mistakes. Any interference will hinder the situation, rather than help it. Stay silent and focus on the more important issues of life.

♉

13 FRIDAY Your objectives occasionally clash with those of somebody else, even though you are used to giving each other the space you need. There could be special factors at the root of the latest conflict, however, and papering over the cracks won't conceal them. Face facts, and then go onto the next stage.

14 SATURDAY Today there is a Full Moon in the fiery sign of Sagittarius. This is certainly not an ideal time for matters relating to clubs, friendships and acquaintances, so try not to impose yourself on others because, if you do, there will be a falling out that you will regret at a later date.

15 SUNDAY This could be a frustrating day. Just when you think you are given the green light to push ahead, something seems to be blocking your path. Never mind, Taurus, turn your attention to more certain, less important things of life. They've probably been hanging around for some time waiting for you to deal with them.

16 MONDAY Certain people may sing your praises, but they could be paying lip service to your ideas as part of a hidden agenda. Call their bluff and see how they back out of something they never intended to pursue in the first place. There's too much at stake for you to go along with hypocrisy or lies.

17 TUESDAY Today Mars enters Pisces and the area of your chart devoted to friends and team activities. It might be a good idea to check out insurance policies and make sure that something hasn't lapsed, because if it should it will give you sleepless nights and that simply won't do, so double-check.

♉

18 WEDNESDAY Be careful and tactful today, particularly when dealing with acquaintances or friends. If you decide to speak your mind, then I'm afraid it's not going to be well received today. If you work as part of a team there may be something that seems to be blocking your progress.

19 THURSDAY You should take a trip today, in spite of a sense of a need that has held you back until now. In some ways it doesn't matter whether you stay or go. However, the astrological set-up makes you realize you cannot dither any longer over something others cope with on a regular basis.

20 FRIDAY One of the most therapeutic things you can do when faced with impossible situations or unreasonable people is to focus on practical tasks. True, these may not be interesting in themselves, but they can bring a feeling of accomplishment just when you need it most.

21 SATURDAY The next couple of days are going to be ones when you need to be realistic about what you want to achieve with relative ease, and that which is beyond your reach. Any differences between yourself and workmates can be cleared up in record time, so make the first move if necessary.

22 SUNDAY Today the Sun will be moving into Cancer and that's the area of your chart which rules the mind, which is going to be much clearer than it has been for a while. Matters relating to brothers and sisters are going to be higher on your list of priorities, but no squabbling please. Furthermore, there'll be lots of new acquaintances entering your scene and some of them will become good friends after a while.

♉

23 MONDAY Loved ones may impede your progress, but tell yourself it is done with the best intentions. Even so, that doesn't mean you can afford to be held back during such a decisive time in your life. The astrological set-up will bring out the commitment and determination needed to do what you know to be right. So be glad that some form of conflict is sometimes the perfect catalyst to force you to focus your ideas and act upon them.

24 TUESDAY Letting your hair down and doing precisely what you please is definitely high on your list of priorities at the moment. Loved ones may be staging a minor mutiny, but you're not doing too badly in the rebellion stakes yourself. There may be a minor re-run today of the events of last week, when you were on your high horse and distracted. But it will be much easier to shrug them off and move on this time. Be nice to friends and not too pushy.

25 WEDNESDAY The stars suggest that over the next couple of days you'll make a fresh beginning where work is concerned. It may also be the case that you are meeting new people in connection with your job and any fresh faces upon the scene should be given your full attention, because they could be lucky for you.

26 THURSDAY Don't rock the boat too much at home, even if you are feeling like letting the cat out of the bag. Count to a hundred and think beautiful thoughts, then throw yourself wholeheartedly into an absorbing project, although this may just be pleasing your loved ones.

♉

27 FRIDAY Right now you have a fascination with new ideas or techniques and some wacky workmates will encourage you. Yet the stars can also give you a distinctly roller-coaster feeling about the way events are turning out. Just remember the old Chinese saying: 'What is high will eventually become low'; the reverse is also true.

28 SATURDAY You're full of wild and way out opinions and you do sometimes hit the bullseye so well that even your sternest critics stand back amazed. However, you can also be rather off the wall with some of your comments. Although this may be your way of getting people's attention, a more moderate approach would be less wearing on your nerves and would keep the atmosphere sweeter.

29 SUNDAY Today Mercury decides to move on into the water sign of Cancer – the area of your chart devoted to local activities – and you'll find it difficult to sit down for even a few moments. Your friends might wonder what on earth's come over you. Never mind, at least your body and mind are being stimulated: it's better than falling asleep for hours on end like some people do. You can never be accused of that. If you've Cancerians in your life and you want to make changes, it might be a good idea to consult them; they'll probably give you a fresh slant on matters.

30 MONDAY Don't leap to conclusions or make extravagant purchases, otherwise you could cause a minor tiff with a close partner who thinks they need to be consulted every step of the way. Whether this is true or not is up to you to decide.

♉

JULY

The Sun this month will be drifting along in the water sign of Cancer until the 22nd. That's the area of your chart devoted to buying and selling, affairs related to brothers, sisters and other relatives. It would be a good idea to keep a pen and pad handy. I've never said that before but these days you seem to be full of inspirational ideas and you don't want them to disappear when you most need them.

On the 23rd, the Sun will be entering Leo and the area of your chart devoted to the home, where there seems to be some feverish activity going on. Of course, it may be that you're simply entertaining friends, or perhaps improving your surroundings: either activity is certainly well starred, that's for sure. If you have a Leo in your life, later on in the month they're going to be a great support to you, either at work or on the home front. Listen to what they have to say.

Mercury will be in Cancer until 13 July, so there's a great deal of coming and going in your life at this time. Perhaps you're finding little excuses to keep on the move, or possibly you're visiting relatives. And talking of family, they're going to be on the telephone quite a lot, I can assure you.

On the 14th, Mercury moves into Leo where it stays until the end of the month. Certainly if you have any Leos in your circle, they're going to be extremely lively and will be great company during this time. Leo, of course, is the area of your chart devoted to home, where minor changes are taking place and visitors drop in quite regularly. However, if you've got a fancy for one of your partner's friends, you should keep that to yourself – otherwise a great deal of unpleasantness could occur, and that would be a great pity.

♉

Venus is in Gemini for the first four days of the month - not very long, but just long enough for you to make up with a relative with whom you are estranged. On the 5th, Venus moves into Cancer, where it stays until late in the month. Your mind seems to be getting calmer and any ideas you have are likely to be well received by the appropriate person. However, there is a slight danger that you may be flirting on the working front and, if so, this could lead to trouble – you've been warned.

Mars is in Pisces all month, so if you have a member of this sign amongst your circle you can expect them to be tense and generally bad tempered. Perhaps you should give them a wide berth for a while. Furthermore, you need to be respectful with your male friends, otherwise there could be a gigantic chasm developing between you and that would be a great pity. You don't like to lose friends now, do you?

The pattern made by the stars seems to be extremely scattered; however, you've got serious work to attend to and you're going to have to dredge up some concentration from somewhere, otherwise mistakes will make you look foolish in the eyes of your colleagues, and maybe even your boss.

In your personal life, too, you can't be bothered spending time with the same old faces. You want novelty, and whether your partner agrees with you or not, you're going to look for it. Oh dear, there could be some tension and bad feeling unless you're very careful. Make sure that you are.

Lastly, with Venus' placing in Cancer, it's likely that you will want to beautify your surroundings and, if so, your excellent taste will be much admired by anyone who visits your home.

♉

1 TUESDAY What you really want is to wrap yourself up protectively and push away all the usual hassles and aggravation. You'll not manage it on this busy day, but make sure you do aim to create an oasis of calm for yourself every so often. Close partners are edgy and determined to pick arguments at every turn. Don't be provoked, but try to harness their energy into cooperative schemes. Keep your deeper feelings to yourself.

2 WEDNESDAY You may feel more confident than you have for a while. Furthermore, those who are closest to you are ready to listen to your ideas and suggestions. They will give you a great deal more affection than they have for quite some time.

3 THURSDAY It is difficult to say whether the changes indicated in the current planetary set-up involve a new approach or extend to a new location as well. Whatever the result, by settling what you can do without at this time will enable you to move quickly and decisively whenever it becomes necessary for you to do so.

4 FRIDAY Whatever close partners are saying, you know you want your own way, no matter what. Try to agree to disagree, or be tolerant of each other's preferences. You must know by this time that nothing can be gained by issuing ultimatums or coming on too strong. Play the game softly and just wend your own way through events. You'll pick up a good deal of praise if you keep your responses muted.

5 SATURDAY Today Venus will be moving into Cancer – the area of your chart connected with brothers and sisters, short

♉

trips and creativity. Furthermore, if you have fallen out with somebody on the working front, you are provided with an excellent opportunity for making up as swiftly as possible. To let things hang around getting stale only makes them worse.

6 SUNDAY The stars are suggesting that you may change your mind more than once about important matters during this day. It might be a good idea to maintain the status quo until this aspect has faded away, because to make decisions now may mean they will have to be undone at a later date.

7 MONDAY Either you can fall in with the wishes of those around you or you can head off in the direction you think best. What you cannot continue to do is to avoid making decisions that may have an impact on a friendship or close association. Once it's done, you'll realize it wasn't such a major problem as you had envisaged.

8 TUESDAY While you may try to sweep everyone along on a wave of enthusiasm, you must be aware that there may be those who quickly lose interest in your pet projects. This is only to be expected, Taurus, so do try not to take this to heart or bear a grudge.

9 WEDNESDAY Those closest to you, both at work and at home, are likely to be in a sober frame of mind. They may, of course, attempt to try and talk some sense into you and won't appreciate it if you insist on behaving elusively. I'm afraid you'll have to stop running and face your detractors, because it's the only way they will appreciate the fact that you have done your best.

♉

10 THURSDAY Now that the watching and waiting are at an end, you are free to let your ideas be known. The aspects today remind you, however, that others may not see your plans in quite the same light as you do. If you feel you're being held back, it's not for selfish or sinister reasons – it's simply because you'll be missed.

11 FRIDAY A parting of the ways need not be nearly so traumatic as you first thought. The stars highlight not just what has gone on before, but great hopes for what happens next. Try not to be affected by someone else's sentimental ways, but remain steadfast in your belief that the best is yet to come.

12 SATURDAY You appear to be daunted by the prospect of all that needs to be done on the financial front. You will continue to be so as long as you insist on struggling on alone. Has it not occurred to you that offers of help are genuine and heartfelt? Don't let foolish pride stand between you and the perfect solution.

13 SUNDAY Today is the day of the Full Moon and it occurs in the sign of Capricorn. That's the area of your chart devoted to higher education, long-distance travelling and your ideals – all of which may be under threat one way or the other. Don't make any important moves for the time being. Allow a couple of days to pass and think again – in that way you'll do the right thing.

14 MONDAY There's a strong suggestion here that many new faces will be entering your social scene. Some will be merely social acquaintances but others could be there to give you a helping hand, or to provide some advice. So make sure

♉

you open up your mind to the words and wisdom that are coming your way, if you are to make the most of your time.

15 TUESDAY Someone else's erratic behaviour means you must decide whether to speak up or shut up. The build up of the aspects today could make it difficult for you to control your emotions. If you must have your say, try to keep it to the absolute minimum necessary. At times like this a show of temper is never a pretty sight.

16 WEDNESDAY It seems that your talents are being used in the best possible way, but you're about to be led into a direction which you've never thought of taking. Tell yourself you will excel at whatever you set out to achieve. Don't be surprised if any off-the-cuff remark or chance encounter changes your life overnight.

17 THURSDAY If you allow others to take advantage of your good nature, you will have no one to blame but yourself. The fact that you are always such a good listener doesn't mean you can expect the same in return. Be very discriminating when choosing a shoulder to cry on. It's important you don't feel belittled or ignored.

18 FRIDAY A close relationship will demand your attention during the days ahead. Of course, things may not run entirely smoothly but you should end up feeling you are spending your time with the right person in the right way. If not, you'll do everyone a favour to face up to the fact once and for all.

19 SATURDAY You really must be careful not to let the fact that so much is going on keep you from tackling boring but

♉

important jobs. Changes may mean that at some point you will alter your direction in life; however, this doesn't mean that it isn't vital to keep up with your duties, obligations and promises.

20 SUNDAY Someone's shortcomings may once have come between you. However, today's aspects suggest you are closer than you ever thought likely. When you look back on this chapter in your life, you'll realize it's one when you learned the value of tolerance.

21 MONDAY It's quite likely that many new people will be coming into your life over the next couple of days or so. Legal matters can be pushed without fear of disappointment, and if you are involved in any kind of study, test or examination it should go well.

22 TUESDAY Because other people are in a highly sociable mood, you may be expected to join them in mixing business with pleasure. Do so without complaining because, after all, they usually give you 100 per cent backing and cooperation.

23 WEDNESDAY Today the Sun will be moving into Leo and the area of your chart devoted to your home, your family and bricks and mortar. Furthermore, it's likely that you'll be bringing friends home at the drop of a hat – but for heaven's sake, ring your partner first, otherwise there'll be some unpleasantness you really don't want – it'll ruin the evening.

24 THURSDAY A tricky relationship needs careful handling. What you must not do is to become too preoccupied with minor problems. They shouldn't be allowed to develop into a

♉

major threat to your peace and happiness. There are two very important words in the English language: 'yes' and 'no'. Use them wisely and well.

25 FRIDAY The emphasis today seems to be on matters related to children, love affairs, sport and socializing. There seems to be a shadow cast over at least one of these areas, perhaps two, but fortunately your ready wit and happy smile may help to lighten things up. But don't rely on this too much, or you may be let down.

26 SATURDAY The day ahead will be challenging and emotional. You want to blaze your own trail at work. Money will come in fairly easily, but your home life will be tense, though relationships will eventually prosper.

27 SUNDAY Everyone else seems rather highly strung, and you could do well to keep working away quietly in the background. The astrological set-up indicates that pulling strings in the background would be far more effective than thumping the table for a day or so. You certainly don't want to cooperate or fit in with somebody else's agenda. However, there's no sense in making a fuss. Just duck out and do your own thing.

28 MONDAY Emotionally you are on tenterhooks - ready to cut restrictive ties and go your own way. But you may also be taken aback if loved ones seem to be in the same rebellious mood. Socially and romantically this is a challenging time for you: you should sort out the wheat from the chaff. Deciding what you really want for yourself while making a commitment is not simple. You will make considered judgements in a couple of days.

♉

29 TUESDAY Today is the day of the New Moon and it occurs in the fiery sign of Leo. That's the area of your chart devoted to home, where there seems to be increased activity. Will it never end, you wonder? It would be quite nice to have your family to yourself from time to time, wouldn't it? But it doesn't look as if it's going to happen yet, I'm afraid.

30 WEDNESDAY Venus has now moved into Leo and therefore you seem to be greatly preoccupied with your home and family – maybe there's some drama going on there. I'm beginning to get suspicious about this, but if this should be the case, somebody's going to have to use some common sense. If it can't be you, then pick the person you know you can trust within the family circle and get them on your side.

31 THURSDAY Unsettling experiences that seem to come out of the blue always accompany certain astrological aspects. Your physical stamina may not be high at this moment because you seem to have been left with a good many chores and not enough help or appreciation. But think positively. You will only have yourself to thank when it all works out well, and you are learning a huge amount about yourself.

AUGUST

The Sun will be drifting through the fiery sign of Leo up until the 23rd. This is the area of your chart devoted to home and family and, to a degree, bricks and mortar too. If you have been considering moving from one area to another, and as long as you've done your homework – in other words you've got a surveyor in to look at the new property – then there's no reason why you shouldn't make the change.

On the 24th, the Sun will be moving into Virgo, the area of your chart denoting children, social life, casual romance and sporting activities. Any, or all, of these can be successful for you now, so be confident when you are participating in them.

Mercury will be in Virgo for the entire month and because of this you may be signing paperwork in connection with off-spring or family matters. The stream of visitors seems to be never-ending and, although you welcome this to begin with, around mid-month you begin to feel a little bit jaded and begin to discourage them. But do so with affection – you don't want to break up long-standing relationships.

Venus will be in Leo until 21 August, so your social activities continue, as do your efforts to beautify your surroundings – buying new furnishings perhaps. Once Venus gets into Virgo on the 22nd, you suddenly decide to break out and enjoy yourself. Well, you've had quite a lot of responsibility lately, so why shouldn't you kick up your heels once in a while? No reason whatsoever, and don't let anyone tell you otherwise. If you are single, you're going to have a string of admirers on the telephone or banging at your door. I don't know what any flatmates or your family will think, but you'll consider this to be flattering and, of course, you're right!

Mars is now in retrograde movement for the whole month as it sails through Pisces, and you could be starting to wonder if it's ever going to let up. Not for quite a while I'm afraid. In the meantime, if you have a Piscean in your life you'll need to make allowances for their erratic behaviour and even, on occasions, downright 'nastiness'. They don't mean to offend you, they're simply opening their mouth without thinking and, of course, we all do that from time to time, don't we? Including you, of course!

1 FRIDAY You're leaping around like a cat on a hot tin roof, determined that no one will interfere with anything you want to do. The truth of the matter is that friends and loved ones are in much the same mood. So everyone's racing around in ever-decreasing circles and getting nowhere fast. Calm down and think serenely about what comes next. Easy to say, difficult to do, but it's the thought that counts!

2 SATURDAY Getting bossy, laying down the law and making more than a few waves can have a rather extraordinary effect. It pushes through barriers at work and clears the deck of useless obstacles. It can also, however, ruffle feathers. You always look stronger emotionally than you really are. You're a great sentimentalist at heart, particularly where your family is concerned, and you do find confrontations rather unsettling.

3 SUNDAY In the old days no one thought of you as a pioneer or an initiator of new schemes, but you have surprised everyone recently with your flow of ideas and plans. Just don't rock the boat too much. The planets, for a few more days, suggest that you'll need to take things slowly, no matter how restless you feel. Remember, there is a time and a season for everything.

4 MONDAY No one doubts that you have a good grasp of the English language, and are more than handy at wielding it at times, but you have so much rushing around to do at the moment that you need to pull in your horns. Persuasion

♉

works better with the volume turned down low and a touch
of flattery thrown in for good measure.

5 TUESDAY Recently any difficulties you may have had at
work, where progress has been tediously slow, gradually
begin to ease and you feel you can push ahead once more.
Take things one step at a time and you really can't go wrong.

6 WEDNESDAY Both at work and at home those closest to
you will have plenty of good imaginative ideas. The question
is, are you going to be quiet and let them explain them to
you? I certainly hope so, because somehow or other you could
benefit.

7 THURSDAY Hopefully you've decided to take your
summer holidays now, because you'll get good value for
money and really be able to relax and let off steam. You may
also have a holiday romance if you're single – of course, don't
even think about it if you've got a partner in tow.

8 FRIDAY Your efforts to keep control of one rather aggra-
vated situation may not have worked as well as expected.
However, half a success is better than none at all. You have
opened your eyes to so many new ideas recently that it is
impossible to put them all into practice instantly. Truth to tell,
you must admit that some of them are pretty cranky anyway.
Put into practice those that are realistic before you leap ahead
with those that are not.

9 SATURDAY All of your hot-headed reckless impulses are
being stifled at the moment with the current planetary set-up.
Use your energy constructively to dig a little deeper into the

♉

background of things. There's a great temptation just to run away from tricky emotional confrontations or financial discussions. But, if you can stand steady you may reach rather inspired compromises and new agreements. Think laterally, but keep walking straight ahead.

10 SUNDAY So much has happened recently that you may be having a minor identity crisis. You cannot decide quite how to appear to other people or, indeed, what you really want. The planets at this time peel off the superficial layers and let you see where you have been compromising or fitting in too much. Once you find yourself, you may be forced to make one or two minor, rather radical decisions, but that will only happen slowly.

11 MONDAY It's important that you ignore certain brilliant get-rich-quick schemes. They are likely to leave you a good deal poorer at a later date. This evening seems set fair for romance, and so, if you're single, doll yourself up and get out into the spotlight, because you never know!

12 TUESDAY Opening up your deeper feelings to yourself, never mind to those you most intimately trust, is never easy. You are probably the most emotionally sensitive sign and prone to being hurt deeply in ways you cannot communicate. But now you need to recognize that you are leaving a good deal of the past behind and moving towards new possibilities. You always approach things in a rather roundabout way; even so, you can do everything you have to do. All you have to do is to believe it.

♉

13 WEDNESDAY Don't be surprised if somebody you are financially dependent upon – your boss or your partner – is a little bit of a disappointment. There's no point in stating the obvious, which is 'I told you so'. The best thing to do is to lend your support, and after a couple of days they'll pick themselves up and start all over again.

14 THURSDAY This will be a grumpy, gritty, rather disruptive day, which will have you in a contradictory mood. You want support, but are flaring up at the drop of a hat. You want to dash off on the longest leash possible, but being told what to do is guaranteed to bring the red mist down. Find yourself an adventure. You won't be able to settle into those boring chores.

15 FRIDAY If you're looking for romance today, and providing you are single, then you should find someone to set your heart racing – well, for a couple of weeks anyway. Mind you, if you are at home, that opposite number of yours will need to keep tabs on you, because you're at your most flirtatious.

16 SATURDAY The aspects are a little bit difficult today and this is a clear indication that people who are closest to you are being over-optimistic, impulsive and extravagant. Somebody's going to have to try a gentle restraining hand and it might just as well be you. If you fail to do so, then I'm afraid their recklessness could rub off on you in an unfortunate way.

17 SUNDAY The stars are in an awkward mood today and you may find progress difficult because you're blocked by others, both at work and at home. No doubt they have sound reasons for doing so – perhaps they imagine you're going off

♉

in the wrong direction – but you will not agree. The best thing to do is to sit down and talk matters through; in that way you might reach an understanding.

18 MONDAY There seem to be some minor changes going on perhaps on the work front. It's possible that there may be new people at work, or perhaps you're signing a new contract, or maybe even going on a business trip, which should prove to be lucrative. All in all, you're starting a happy phase.

19 TUESDAY This is a day when you can chase money that you're owed – providing, of course, you use charm – because other people will capitulate very quickly. This evening keep a high profile particularly if you are unattached, because you may meet someone rather special.

20 WEDNESDAY Those around you on this particular day may not measure up to your high standards, but do take care not to hold this against them for one reason or another. If you ignore their opinions and suggestions, then matters will go from bad to worse.

21 THURSDAY Do try to keep in the thick of things over the next day or so, especially when it comes to going out on any sort of social occasion. It is likely that you're going to be spoiled for choice, so you can have as much fun as you want. Romance is in the air, so you should have little to complain about, particularly during the evening hours.

22 FRIDAY Today Venus will be moving into Virgo, the area of your chart devoted to matters related to children, casual romance, creativity and generally everything that is

♉

lighthearted in life. Your companions will be delighted with your mood and will come away vowing to see you again as soon as possible.

23 SATURDAY The spirit of adventure in you strikes when you're making plans for future socializing. Furthermore, you'll be prepared to travel quite a distance in order to enjoy yourself, or perhaps because you're looking for romance – and why not? Those who come from foreign lands will hold a particular appeal for you.

24 SUNDAY Today the Sun will be moving into Virgo and the area of your chart devoted to creativity, sports, children and the arts in general. If you've got any good ideas, jot them down on a piece of paper. Never mind what other people say; after all, it could be the beginning of an exciting new novel – you never know.

25 MONDAY Your concentration is spot on. Therefore, if you need to make any important decisions you shouldn't hesitate to do so. However, it is likely that a social occasion may either not come up to your expectations or could be cancelled altogether. You need a contingency plan that can be adopted at the last moment.

26 TUESDAY Those of you who have friends or contacts in other countries are likely to be hearing from them. For others, it may be that you're taking some kind of break or holiday – and you couldn't have chosen a better time for getting away. Never mind the weather, it's the company you're keeping that counts.

27 WEDNESDAY Today, other people's ideas may very well change your outlook on life. This evening it's likely that you're going to something special and everything should run smoothly. By the time today is through you can be quite sure that everyone concerned will have smiles on their faces.

28 THURSDAY Mercury continues in a retrograde movement in Virgo for quite some time after today, so you may as well get used to its influence. What could this be? Well, it does help your creativity. It is good, too, if you're travelling for the sake of your job, and if you're involved in any kind of litigation it should go your way. So be confident – that's the way to go.

29 FRIDAY Today you're going to be spoiled for choice when it comes to opportunities for romance and having fun. Be selective, but also be loyal. If this means choosing between something fairly exciting with a good friend, or something wild and crazy with colleagues or acquaintances, then you'd be very well advised to go with the former.

30 SATURDAY You're at your most charming, affable, creative and sociable. Not surprisingly the opposite sex will be queuing up for your attention. Somebody may be acting in an objectionable way, probably only to get attention, so be on your guard.

31 SUNDAY Your loved ones may have long-held plans that they will be reluctant to change at the last moment just to please you. Unless, of course, your ideas are so exciting they simply can't be ignored. Luckily, this evening you're in a lighthearted mood, so instead of trying to make your own luck, you'll be ready to take life as it comes.

♉

SEPTEMBER

During the month the Sun will be travelling through the earthy sign of Virgo up until the 22nd, and that is the area of your chart which rules creativity, sports, partying, children and casual romance. Can't be bad.

However, on the 23rd, the Sun will be moving into Libra and then, I'm afraid, you will have to put away your dancing shoes and start to be more serious. There are decisions that you need to be making of a professional nature and also on the home front, and to ignore this fact would be foolhardy, not to mention making you extremely unpopular.

Mercury will be in Virgo all month and will finally resume direct movement on the 20th. That's a relief, isn't it? You've had to be so careful where your paperwork is concerned, but now you can just relax and jog along in your normal fashion.

Venus is also in Virgo until the 15th. However, on 16 September Venus will move into Libra – a little reprimand from the stars that you've really got to get down to the nitty-gritty of work before somebody realizes how slapdash and lazy you've been recently. Furthermore, you need to watch your health too: there will be a tendency for you to over-indulge like crazy late in the month and if you find yourself suffering from a permanent hangover, well, you'll only have yourself to blame.

Mars continues its retrograde movement in Pisces and so if you have a member of this sign in your circle, don't be surprised if they run rings around you, or come to you for help because they're so confused. Fortunately they've picked the right person, because the typical Bull is usually very practical and down-to-earth and you can impart some wisdom to them, if you care to of course. Fortunately the planet resumes direct movement on the 27th, so you can begin to relax and take a wider view of things, as opposed to becoming obsessed as all Bulls can be from time to time.

The pattern made by the stars is a rather odd one. There's precious little going on in the zenith part of your chart – maybe your priorities have changed from your professional duties. However, in the lower right hand side of your chart the aspects are looking pretty promising, maybe because Venus is in Libra and that is throwing a rosy glow over work, health and your normal routine, which turns out to be far more pleasant and dramatic than you would have expected, mainly because you are asked to mix business with pleasure on several occasions and, of course, as a Bull no one can hold you back where there seems to be good food and free drink available!

1 MONDAY Today the stars could be frustrating you one way or another. There may be arguments with people you're financially dependent upon, whether it be your boss or your partner. However, to upset anyone on this particular day could lead to a great deal of bad feeling for some time to come, so please stop it.

2 TUESDAY Today the stars will help you to move about unimpeded. Furthermore, it will be easy for you to express the way you feel, or what you think, and you shouldn't hesitate to do so before the aspects change.

3 WEDNESDAY Your energy and enthusiasm know no bounds concerning a creative project or work, but you may not have somebody's blessing. You're right not to allow anything to get in your way, but watch out. The stars are in a difficult mood and there's a danger you'll allow a pleasure to become an obsession.

4 THURSDAY Make it clear that you need to distance yourself from those who think their petty problems should be your main concern. With the current aspects today, you should have no doubt as to whose needs come first – yours.

5 FRIDAY There's a rather serious feel about this particular 24-hour period. It's certainly one that you can use constructively for making important decisions. An older person will be handing on some useful advice, so make sure you pay attention.

6 SATURDAY If you've been clever enough to book yourself a late holiday, then you're not only going to get good value, but you'll have the time of your life too. Those of you who are waiting on results from any kind of examination will be well satisfied with your efforts. It looks then as if there is going to be reason for celebration one way or the other.

7 SUNDAY There is an indication that provides you with a happy, cooperative glow where professional matters are concerned. Furthermore, there is a strong possibility that you'll meet someone rather special while going about your daily routine, so keep those eyes peeled.

8 MONDAY Money that is owed could come rolling in. What's more, you can spend a little, provided you do so sensibly and cautiously. This evening is a rather pleasant time and the chances of romance certainly look promising, so stay alert.

♉

9 TUESDAY It's always difficult to make decisions when situations themselves are on the move. But, with so much happening so quickly, you really have no choice other than to go ahead with what you hope is best and leave working out the fine details to a later date.

10 WEDNESDAY This is the day of the Full Moon and it occurs in the water sign of Pisces. That's the area of your chart devoted to team effort, club activities and, to a degree, new objectives. Old friends will be handing out some wise advice and, although you may initially object, you can resurrect it at a later date.

11 THURSDAY Today the stars suggest there could be some minor changes in connection with your job. Many of you will be signing on the dotted line as contracts are emphasized as, indeed, is travel. Where the latter's concerned, this could, directly or indirectly, lead to romance.

12 FRIDAY No one will thank you for making a fuss, but an alarm bell seems to be ringing in connection with your home and family. The planets will raise your awareness of other people's moods, and you should step in quickly and quietly to avert an unnecessary drama.

13 SATURDAY The stars present you with a frustrating feel about the day. No doubt you'll be itching to push ahead with at least one important project or relationship, but for reasons that seem to be a little bit elusive you are unable to do so. It might be a good idea to use this evening to rest for a change – you probably need an early night.

♉

14 SUNDAY While you are bemoaning the fact that you are tied to one spot, someone is making plans to give you a taste of freedom and adventure you yearn for. If and when an unusual invitation arrives, don't think twice. Say yes. You have to move fast and travel light, but this is an opportunity too good to miss.

15 MONDAY The fact that little is being said about your personal professional achievements doesn't mean you've lost the magic touch. Colleagues and loved ones have grown so used to your consistent high standards, it really is the case of no news is good news. The world knows you're doing fine, and so should you.

16 TUESDAY Today Venus will be moving into Libra and the area of your chart devoted to work, health and your relationships with colleagues – all of which seem to be on a high. However, don't get too inflated, otherwise you may be seen as a 'show off'; nothing could be further from the truth, as you and I both know.

17 WEDNESDAY This is one of those times when your efforts are best used doing what you least want to do. This may mean you have to tackle obligations to certain individuals, but there are other matters of a deeply personal nature which, once dealt with, will both ease your mind and greatly relieve a persistent burden.

18 THURSDAY You may think money matters are a problem, but it is the underlying tension between you and someone close that you must deal with fairly fast. You have undervalued a relationship and it may take a long time to recover;

♉

you must accept that it is not only your opinion that counts. Listen and learn.

19 FRIDAY Something which seemed too far-fetched is becoming a reality and is occupying your mind. In fact, surprise developments are about to prove that anything is possible if your attitude is flexible and your convictions sound. Forget the obvious and conventional – innovation and originality hold the key.

20 SATURDAY You're relieved that Mercury finally resumes direct movement today, therefore from hereon in you needn't worry about travelling from place to place, signing paperwork or dealing with legal matters. All these can be done with alacrity. Furthermore, if you have a Virgo or a Gemini in your life and there has been trouble recently, you will be able to sort it out now. The sooner the better!

21 SUNDAY Other people may doubt you have sufficient knowledge to speculate on a deal that contains an element of risk. You know, however, that you must sometimes let intuition be your guide, even when the odds seem stacked against you. Just be selective about which advice to take on board and which to ignore.

22 MONDAY Where career matters are concerned there's a strong chance that you are being over-optimistic. Identify the pitfalls that exist, there are bound to be at least one or two, and when you have faced them you will know what your next move should be.

♉

23 TUESDAY Today the Sun will be moving into the airy sign of Libra and the area of your chart devoted to health, which is thriving, work, which is enjoyable, and the company of work-mates, who are certainly making you laugh. All in all, you've got a good day so make the most of it.

24 WEDNESDAY Today may be a bit disorganized, particularly if you are going on a short trip, which could be uncomfortable, difficult or result in delays. This 24-hour period should be spent quietly, marking time and smelling the roses rather than being too adventurous.

25 THURSDAY Slowly as the next few days pass you'll begin to smell success on the wind. Complications of the past slowly evaporate, but don't expect it to happen overnight as it is not going to.

26 FRIDAY Today there is a New Moon and it occurs in the airy sign of Libra and this should make for a very positive and constructive day. If you have been stuck in a rut recently this is a great time for making a new start. Why not let go of all those dull and irritating things from the past and embrace all the new and exciting things you have been meaning to get round to doing for so long?

27 SATURDAY If your efforts to convince friends or colleagues that they are on the wrong track seem not to have been taken seriously, don't give in to the idea that it means they haven't been listening. They have, but until situations themselves change they may find it hard to heed even the best advice.

♉

28 SUNDAY Without knowing why, you may feel restless or over-excited and you must not lose sight of a loved one's need for stability. Your current mood will soon pass and by the end of it you may be embarrassed at having created a fuss. You may have to think fast in order to avoid a dispute everyone could well do without.

29 MONDAY Hopefully this is not a time when you have to sign an important document, or involve yourself with any legal matter, or travel any distance. If this is unavoidable then make sure you double check all your arrangements in order to avoid problems which seem to be strewn across your path.

30 TUESDAY Through no fault of your own the best-laid plans do go awry and you'll be forced to think on your feet today. What you cannot see at this stage are ways in which this will benefit you in terms of your work and reputation. The next few days will stretch you to a point where you have to rely on untapped skills. Look at this period as the chance to prove to everyone, including yourself, what a versatile person you really are.

OCTOBER

The Sun will be drifting along in Libra until the 23rd, which is the area of your chart connected with sheer hard slog and health problems. You must definitely make sure that when you get home from your toil that you rest up, and only keep company with people who make you laugh because this is good medicine and helps you to let off steam which, my goodness me, you certainly need to do.

♉

On the 24th, the Sun will be moving into Scorpio and that, of course, is your opposite sign, so you may have to consider other people far more than you usually do. Don't think they won't thank you at a later date because they will; just don't drop heavy hints and demand that they kiss your feet, or even buy you a present!

Mercury will be in Virgo during the first week, so you will be attracted to intellectual pastimes and, furthermore, will want to travel as much as possible to see friends, so the further away they live the better it will be as far as you are concerned.

On the 7th, Mercury moves into Libra, and that's the area of your chart devoted to health matters, among other things. So if you're feeling a little peaky or tired, it might be a good idea just to give your body a good rest and, of course, nourish it without stuffing yourself to the point where you feel sick – many Taureans do tend to do this, believe it or not!

On 24 October, Mercury will be moving in Scorpio and because of this there'll be rumours of contracts on the working front that will be beneficial for all and sundry. It might be a good idea to socialize a bit more with colleagues so that you can swap information you've been given. It is only by doing this will you find out the truth, and then you'll know exactly how to act.

Venus will be drifting along in Libra until 9 October. This is the area of your chart devoted to relationships with workmates, which should be good, and health, which may suffer from over indulgence from time to time – but being a Bull you can't really help it, can you?

Venus moves into your opposite sign Scorpio on the 10th, so at least there's a cosy happy glow over your relationships with other people. In fact, some of you may be meeting the 'love of your life' at this time, so do make sure you're looking good, feeling good and are as affable and as friendly as possible. You wouldn't like to miss out on this now, would you?

Mars will be coasting along in Pisces, the area of your chart devoted to friends. This planet seems to be having a rather long stay in this sign and, therefore, any bad feelings that exist between you and other people have probably been going on for some time. Hopefully, soon, you'll be able to bring this to an end or if you don't, somebody else should. If you are handed the olive branch, for heaven's sake take it – you'll regret it later if you don't.

The pattern made by the stars is a very scattered one, which means that it'll be difficult for you to concentrate on any one area of life. There's too much happening to grab your attention and, of course, this keeps you very busy – which you love. Sitting around doing nothing is not your idea of fun except on rare occasions, such as festive periods, birthdays, etc., when, of course, it is permissible.

It looks as if you're going to learn quite a lot during October, so be prepared to sit at somebody else's knee and listen to what they have to say.

1 WEDNESDAY You may be ready to suggest sweeping changes within the home or family, but not everyone has an instant grasp of the situation. Perhaps you are forgetting the feelings of those who like things the way they are. If you go too fast, you'll leave them behind and might even lose them altogether. What a shame.

2 THURSDAY Fulfil duties and obligations by all means, but don't let them rule your life. You have a tendency to become a martyr to the cause that may turn out to be a five-minute wonder. No one is asking you to go back on your word. Don't go one step further than you need until more questions have been answered.

3 FRIDAY This is a 24-hour period when there could be a lot of upheaval and change, particularly where a partnership and working affairs are concerned. You can be flexible and adaptable when you deem necessary and I think this is one of those periods when it most definitely is, so see what you can do.

4 SATURDAY There's a certain impetus to matters related to further education, foreigners and travel. Mind you, do take care that you are not too impulsive where these aspects to life are concerned. If you slow down just a touch, you'll find that it will be easier to spot potential mistakes, and so prevent them from impeding your progress.

5 SUNDAY If colleagues and companions try to rule the roost, remember you are under no-one's power but your own. Conflict or controversy may leave you feeling edgy or ill at ease, but you must strengthen your resolve to make decisions and stick to them. Be strong, be decisive, but most important of all, be quick.

6 MONDAY You're in a mood to say what you like, while certain individuals may retaliate in kind. Because you feel especially buoyant, you'll probably want to clear the air of something that has been left unsaid and unexplained. Don't think of being defeated or shouted down. Your ability to bounce back will see you through.

7 TUESDAY Today Mercury will be moving into Libra, the area of your chart devoted to health matters, which are good, and your relationships with workmates, which are not quite so hot. Try to work on the latter because only if there's peace and harmony on the work front will the team get on with what needs to be done. You don't want to be held responsible for holding things up now, do you?

8 WEDNESDAY Stick your neck out by all means, but don't be surprised if you begin to feel you're being penalized by someone involved in your financial affairs. Of course, you are right not to toe the line if you see great flaws and failings in a major deal or set-up. Your ideals and principles count above all else.

9 THURSDAY There's a certain amount of movement and change at work. Should you be given the opportunity to travel for the sake of professional matters then grab it with both hands, because it can prove illuminating and will lead to greater things.

10 FRIDAY Today Venus moves into Scorpio – the area of your chart which rules partnerships; existing relationships are certainly thriving at the moment. However, if you're fancy free, then you have a couple of weeks when it's likely that you'll meet someone special on the romantic front, so make sure you look good and keep your eyes open.

11 SATURDAY Your usual methodical tactics and techniques may go by the board as you learn to become more of a jack of all trades. Challenges presented by way of a set-to between the planets could open all sorts of possibilities if you break

♉

away from the routines and patterns of the past. Your skills
and talents are more broadly based than you and other people
realize. If you've always wanted to try something new, now's
your chance.

12 SUNDAY The stars seem to suggest that when it comes to
a new romance you may be anything but straightforward.
Possibly you already have a partner and are especially prone
to temptation, which will be hard to resist. Nevertheless, if
you love that other person enough then you will be able to
manage. If you don't – well, it's best that you find out now.

13 MONDAY It seems you are thinking one thing and a loved
one is thinking quite the opposite. But even so, if you put
your heads together, you can come up with a scheme that
works. Try to show how well your unconventional approach
to many of life's problems can help. The ordinary or mundane
will get you nowhere.

14 TUESDAY You'd be ill advised to make any important
moves right now, especially signing documents where money
matters are concerned. Furthermore, while travelling around
this evening, you may lose something precious; it would be a
good idea to leave any little treasures at home – why take
chances?

15 WEDNESDAY Despite the risks involved, you seem keen
to extend your talents further afield. The stars are urging you
to take a chance, while one planet is highlighting the potential
problems that may impede your progress. Be decisive, be
inventive, and don't be too proud to back down the minute
you feel something's wrong.

♉

16 THURSDAY Disagreement over love or money must not be allowed to cause a rift. The planets are at odds with one another, but that does not mean you have to wage war with someone. It would be far better to analyse any mistakes made by you or someone else and to learn from them. Avoid any hasty thinking or thoughtless action.

17 FRIDAY It's likely that someone close to you is either feeling depressed, ill-used or simply weighed down with responsibility. Should you sense that this is the case, see what you can do to alleviate this state of affairs. They'll be forever grateful to you and besides, it's the only decent thing to do anyway.

18 SATURDAY Slipping and slithering into a day with a head full of sea fog, it's unlikely that you'll make sensible decisions for a while, so just have a break until you can clear the debris out of the way. Financially, you need to be more careful than usual, just for a day or two anyway. So keep your chequebook shut, leave all those credit cards at home and try to avoid temptation.

19 SUNDAY You're getting to resemble that air sign, Libra, more and more as you circle around problem areas trying to make up your mind what to do! Yet, no matter which side you view it from, it all seems like a big question mark. 'When in doubt, do nowt' and for you at the moment, this is probably the wisest move. In a couple of days you'll have found the magical solution and be able to start bouncing back.

20 MONDAY 'What you see is what you get' describes your temperament at this moment in time. You're never one to hide your light away under a bushel or keep your opinions to yourself, but for once you have a secretive smile which makes you look enigmatic and cool. No one could guess what's going on behind your mask – why should they? You fully intend to let one idea hatch out in its own good time, and then you'll reveal all.

21 TUESDAY Protect what is valuable in your life. You want to be more secretive or hidden for a day or so until you see how the land lies. There have been so many terrible upheavals recently that it is somewhat tricky to get a clear sense of perspective for the future. However, you're about to fall into a period ripe with potential, so you need to establish your agenda.

22 WEDNESDAY Make a dedicated effort to sparkle at work or in your community. In certain circumstances it will take an effort and you may have to please everyone else rather than yourself, but you will benefit ultimately if you can create a good impression. The astrological set-up at the moment is making you inclined to build brick walls around yourself and to keep companions at arm's length. Let your feelings show more.

23 THURSDAY There's an indication today that you may be introduced into a new circle of friends, amongst whom you are likely to find at least one admirer. Get out and socialize this evening, because you are likely to meet some interesting new people who can not only make you laugh, but can also help you in some way.

♉

24 FRIDAY Today is the day when the Sun will be moving into Scorpio. That is your opposite number, and so it's likely that you will have to bow to the wishes and needs of other people rather than your own. You must try not to resent this, although it may be difficult. You can do it, especially with your iron will.

25 SATURDAY Today Mercury follows the Sun into the sign of Scorpio, so there are likely to be many changes in your friendship circle, and also possibly where romance is concerned. There's a possibility, too, that you may be temporarily infatuated with a foreigner. Well, there's no reason why you shouldn't be, but don't expect the relationship to last overly long – it won't.

26 SUNDAY You have a bubbling sense of anticipation for celebrations that seem to lie ahead. You are at a peak career-wise, and over the next couple of days you may find influential people happy to praise your talents in the weeks to come. However, you seem rather stuck over one immediate muddle in your everyday working life. Don't force the pace, it may be that a new factor will emerge which will totally change your outlook.

27 MONDAY The stars suit you today since you can skip around stimulating company, throwing around your brighter ideas. But everyone seems flustered and inattentive, so you may feel pushed back onto your own resources more than you might like. Just rise gracefully above the trivial concerns and look ahead. Sorting out home and family becomes much easier in the near future.

ŏ

28 TUESDAY Those who are closest to you may be a little bit over-confident or over-optimistic. Take what they say with a large pinch of salt and enquire as to whether they have done any real research. I think you'll find they have not.

29 WEDNESDAY If you feel as if the ground is starting to shift beneath your feet, don't start getting worried about earthquakes. Maybe you have been a little bit too self-contained or enclosed. What is happening is that you are, subconsciously at least, trying to shake yourself into action. Too much security can be suffocating. Although changes and risk can be frightening, they also bring new life.

30 THURSDAY Love could be in the air, which may sound strange in the midst of a rather disruptive influence, but your emotional life has been on such a roller coaster ride in recent days that you have become used to fun and turmoil running side by side. Nothing that really belongs to you, or is meant to be, will disappear. You could not throw it away even if you wanted to, so go with the flow and have trust.

31 FRIDAY It is likely that you'll be making new contacts, acquaintances and friends. Some of them will be extremely useful to you, while others may teach you a great deal about yourself and other people.

NOVEMBER

This month the Sun will be coasting along through the water sign of Scorpio until the 22nd, so once more your close relationships, both at work and at home, are highlighted. Some of you may even be forming very lucrative personal

♉

partnerships – so don't hesitate, jump in feet first and there will be a safety net, I can assure you.

On the 23rd, the Sun will be moving into Sagittarius and that's the area of your chart devoted to matters related to banking, new aspirations which you want to adopt, friends and contacts, and it looks as if you're going to be extremely hectic for the latter part of November and you'll enjoy all the activity.

Mercury will be in Scorpio until the 11th. As that's the area of your chart devoted to partners and close relationships, there seems to be quite a lot of novelty and a certain amount of change going on, but nothing too drastic. On the 12th, Mercury will move into Sagittarius – the area of your chart devoted to friends, acquaintances, team effort and, to a degree, projects that are stood in your path. This is likely to be an extremely sociable time, so don't reject chances to enjoy yourself because if you do you will certainly live to regret it.

On 3 November Venus will also be moving into Sagittarius, reinforcing the sociability of this time. Mind you, don't go home late too often from your work, otherwise that partner of yours will begin to object – and who can blame them?

Venus will move into Capricorn on the 27th, the area of your chart related to foreign travel, high inspiration and perhaps, too, the possibility of meeting someone who comes from abroad and someone you're likely to feel quite romantic about. However, this is unlikely to be a long-lived romance so please don't take it too seriously, otherwise you'll get hurt and that would be a shame.

Mars continues in Pisces all month and that's the area of your chart devoted to friendship and the defining of your goals and objectives in life. However, a certain amount of tension can be expected because of Mars' temperament, so do

♉

take things easy and in that way you'll reach the right decision – that's what you need to do, of course.

The pattern made by the stars is a rather odd one, because
the majority of the planets, bar two, are above the horizon.
Because of this there's a clear indication that you are going to
be at your most ambitious. Mind you, you do have thoughts
of travel too, maybe booking a holiday, perhaps immediately
after the Christmas period. Lucky you, if you're going to have
any money left at this time of the year, and if you have, well,
all I can say to you is, well done!

1 SATURDAY With flags waving and banners flying, you are
striding ahead and making sure that special people in your
life know of your presence and opinions. Even if you have to
turn everything upside down, you're clearly going to cause a
stir. Remember to keep kindness in mind if you are going to
be honest, since the blunt truth is not always digestible without a sugar coating to make it slide down.

2 SUNDAY There is a possibility that Lady Luck will be on
your side where cash matters are concerned. Of course, some
of you will be getting an early Christmas present but, either
way, it's a promising day. This evening romance looks fun,
flirtatious, but not too serious, so keep your feet on the
ground.

3 MONDAY You and I both know that you have spoken your
mind and now it is time to allow other people to respond to
you. If they are unwilling or unable to alter their approach or
come across sensibly, then there is nothing further you can do.
You may just as well cruise along happily, reassured that your
conscience is absolutely clear.

ɒ

4 TUESDAY Today seems to be devoted to children, socializing to a degree, and romance. In at least one of these areas there may be a disappointment, but luckily you are the type of person who bounces back quickly and so are unlikely to stay depressed for overly long.

5 WEDNESDAY There seems to be a great deal of movement and change: possibly you're mixing business with pleasure, bearing in mind that the festive period is only around the corner. If so, you will be having the time of your life.

6 THURSDAY You're still pondering on how to cope with one work situation which seems to have you perplexed at the present. Your self-confidence needs a determined shake-up so that you can fly back into the activity at your usual frantic pace again. Impetuous decisions should be avoided for the next couple of days, but in general you know you need to get back in tip-top form and get moving again.

7 FRIDAY As far as you are concerned people are either in your affections or out of them. Your feelings are intense and are either fiercely possessive or switched off altogether. However, maybe you are being asked to find a better balance between more detached acquaintances and closer loved ones. There's definitely room in your life for both, you know.

8 SATURDAY Today you may have a way of playing your own worst enemy so it might be a good idea for you to shelve anything important for the time being. However, getting out this evening and letting off steam won't do you any harm at all.

♉

9 SUNDAY You're at your most restless today and it may be difficult for you to decide how you are going to spend your time. If so, why not allow friends to take control? Should you decide to go along with their suggestions, you will be enjoying yourself and getting the maximum out of life too.

10 MONDAY If someone has turned their back on you recently, or undermined your trust in their loyalty, then you need to avoid resentment. Getting your own back or feeling vengeful is a waste of time, since it generally hurts you more than it does anybody else, and locks you into a very difficult situation that should be written off as history. There's a good deal of social fun on the horizon which could keep you more than occupied, so start sprucing yourself up.

11 TUESDAY It's likely that you're feeling more confident and secure, and in the next few days you will be forming a new relationship and ties which will support you and your ideas for some time to come. Regarding old alliances, it is likely that you will have to decide very soon whether you can cope with them, or whether they are really necessary or not. I don't think it's likely that you'll be able to change anybody.

12 WEDNESDAY Today Mercury will be moving into Sagittarius. This is the area of your chart devoted to team effort, friendship, acquaintances and your goals in life. These may change in a minor way but nothing that is going to floor you, so you can stick to your game plan.

13 THURSDAY Someone may stop you completely in your tracks by saying just what you did not want to hear. But don't be put off by their manner and intentions, instead sift the

♉

information and see if you can dredge anything of value out of it. On occasions, helpful hints turn up from the least expected quarters and not always in their obvious packaging. Snapping back too quickly before you've had time to deliberate would not be wise.

14 FRIDAY It looks as if you're tearing around in an effort to finish work before the festive period arrives, but don't you think you're being a little bit premature? No, perhaps not, seeing as you are a Taurus. However, you may come to the decision fairly soon that you may not be able to cope with the duties you have taken on and, if necessary, you will have to admit it.

15 SATURDAY There seems to be a great deal of activity going on behind the scenes. Maybe you've been asked to keep a secret and you're finding it difficult to do so. But you must keep faith with the person concerned, otherwise you'll be storing up a great deal of trouble for the future.

16 SUNDAY Today the stars suggest that the winds of change are upon you. You are filled with fresh enthusiasm, hope and self-awareness. This in turn will lead to a more forceful and optimistic approach to life. What you need to do before making any important moves is to rationalize the situation rather than consider it as a problem, especially if you believe it to be hopeless. This is an opportunity that can eventually lead to fulfilment.

17 MONDAY Accept all offers of help gratefully and don't be suspicious or dismissive, because it's not as you had hoped. Every little helps. Genuine friends are difficult to find, especially at the present time, so you need to treasure loyalty when it appears. You will need to reorganize your schedule very soon because the pressures of exciting personal projects are mounting.

18 TUESDAY Too many chores or a head full of conflicting thoughts and ideas may have you examining the ground underneath your feet rather closely. Certainly, you have to keep a watchful eye on practical matters, financial ones especially, because there are opportunities around which may slide by if you are not wide awake. But you will also need to give yourself the chance to relax from time to time. Try delegating more.

19 WEDNESDAY Information picked up along the way may help you to see things differently. Impulsive stars are encouraging you to take a risk. Although you may not feel especially lucky at the moment, remember even a rank outsider can win. So pluck up your courage and use your brave streak that others envy and admire.

20 THURSDAY This is an important day where you try to balance the flashes of genius with reality. You must fight to free yourself from any kind of insecurity or phobia related to long-term prospects or finances in your professional life. The only enemy you have is yourself, so don't let your imagination work overtime.

21 FRIDAY Anyone who thinks you can be trampled under foot is in for a surprise. Your image may portray you as caring and generous, which no doubt you are, but you are a lot else beside that. A show of temper will fade as quickly as it flares up, but not before everyone has learned what a forceful person you really are.

22 SATURDAY There may have been some sort of intrigue going on, but you're in a position to force everything out into the open as far as work or health matters are concerned right now. Don't be hard on those who have been feeding rumours and fanning the flames of unrest. Without them you will never have been forced to lead instead of follow, and you wouldn't have learned all you know now. Make use of every bit of information received and create something remarkable for the future.

23 SUNDAY Today the Sun will be moving into Sagittarius and that's the area of your chart devoted to friendship and team effort. Furthermore, you seem to be extremely popular on the working front and if invitations for fun come in, then for heaven's sake accept them; if you happen to be fancy free they could lead to romance.

24 MONDAY There's no point in taking a tough line if you're likely to capitulate in the end. True, things have gone far enough and a fragile set-up will break down unless guidelines are observed or a code of practice followed. The stars are illuminating qualities that set you apart from the rest. Why not use them?

25 TUESDAY A cash crisis must be averted if all your hard work is to pay off. Although you may know the steps you need to take, you mustn't charge ahead and do just what you like. Take into account the feelings of those who have shared your load. They might have very different views from your own.

26 WEDNESDAY Do not put your efforts into a project that shows signs of dying on its feet. Only an injection of your own brand of energy and imagination can save it. It would be a pity to see something fail when it has such a following. Just don't think you can do everything yourself – you can't, and you shouldn't even try. Get help.

27 THURSDAY No one crowds you into a corner when you want to fly away. You have an electric energy that fizzles, sparks and pops when you feel that you need some more elbowroom. Companions are at arm's length and they want to get a good deal closer to you. If you feel the same way then it's about time somebody speaks up.

28 FRIDAY With your sweetest smile at the ready, you are charming all the right people at work or when socializing. You may have an ulterior motive, but others will never notice. Just make sure you are giving yourself a chance to relax as well. The planets are hinting at a way to unshackle one restraining situation.

29 SATURDAY You may be receiving some kind of reward or even promotion. There may be times when colleagues will be envious or simply pleasantly surprised. But whatever occurs it's going to be all to the good.

30 SUNDAY A tough routine at work at the moment means you could feel life is getting a touch unbalanced, so embrace any chance to let your hair down. Be mildly outrageous, if it feels good, with loved ones or friends. They can be rebellious when it suits them, so you might as well have your own moment of freedom as well. Slow down enough for one

♉

in-depth conversation. You will emerge enriched and with a gem of wisdom.

DECEMBER

The Sun will be coasting along in the fiery sign of Sagittarius up until the 21st, and that is the area of your chart devoted to matters related to banking, shared resources and the maintaining of goals.

On the 22nd, the Sun will move into Capricorn and the area of your chart which deals with matters related to abroad, so possibly you're thinking of flying off to sunny climes during the Christmas holidays – and why not, you will thoroughly enjoy yourself as well as getting good value for money. However, even if you are staying at home, it's unlikely you'll be spending Christmas in the comfort of your own home. It's likely that you'll have plenty of chances to enjoy yourself with friends.

Mercury continues to sizzle along in the fiery sign of Sagittarius for the first couple of days, after which it sails on into earthy Capricorn where it will stay until the 30th, making this a good period for money matters – as long as you don't take too many risks or let go of the purse strings. Unfortunately, Mercury goes into retrograde movement on the 17th; hopefully you're not travelling on this day, but if you are you'd better double check your passports and luggage or there might be one almighty mess up if you're not careful.

Venus will be in Capricorn until the 20th – an earth sign like your good self. If you have anyone in your circle born under this sign they're going to be keeping a very high profile. It will be hard for you to turn off your ambitions at this time of the year, but if you don't you're not going to be very popular I can assure you.

On the 21st, Venus will be moving on into Aquarius and that is the zenith point of your chart, so even though it is the end of the year you could be spending it in the company of people you meet through your professional life. However, it might be a good idea to check with your partner because you really don't want them sick to death of you talking business, especially over the Christmas period, do you?

Mars continues in Pisces up until 16 December. Therefore, there could be some squabbles and tension, not only at work but also within your friendship circle, and that would be a great pity. Your partner could be getting fed up with all this wrangling that's been going on for so long now, and somebody's got to call it to a halt: it might as well be you.

On the 17th, Mars will be moving into Aries and that's a secretive side to your chart, which could mean that you're feeling a little under the weather. Maybe you've picked up some germs whilst socializing and you won't be welcome if visiting other people's houses. In fact, it may be that you'll have to spend the holiday time at home. Not that there's anything seriously wrong with you, but you do feel the need to recuperate and rest up and if that is the way you feel then, quite frankly, you should listen to those instincts of yours – they very rarely serve you wrong.

1 MONDAY Over the next day or so opportunities should arise to put right a number of persistent problems or dilemmas. Whilst some will be relatively straightforward, others will demand a combination of charm, persuasion, insight and, most of all, the perspective that only your intuition can give. It will be a good time for paying attention to your diet and exercise before the Christmas period really gets going.

2 TUESDAY Not only should your feelings guide you, those instincts could deal with the power struggles more handily than pure logic. If partners don't respond to reason or gentle persuasion, just give them time. Very soon both your confidence and control will have returned, leaving former critics trying to keep up with you.

3 WEDNESDAY Mercury will be moving into the earthy sign of Capricorn and that's the area of your chart devoted to long-distance travelling, so it's quite likely that if you're not actually abroad yourself, you may be entertaining people from strange lands and, of course, is this is a good idea. Why not?

4 THURSDAY With the Moon in Aries at the moment, now is a time to keep busy and not let the grass grow under your feet. Sometimes it is only too easy for you to become withdrawn or depressed if you haven't got anything stimulating on the go, so keep focused on the practical matters in hand and don't wander off into daydreams.

5 FRIDAY Those you are financially dependent upon may be stressed and argumentative. See what you can do to give them some backing and try to entice them so that they really can relax. The old hormones are jumping around this evening: literally anything could happen, and it probably will!

6 SATURDAY Out on the social scene you look assured, almost sophisticated. Only those who know you intimately can see the ebbs and flows of your moods. Just as you decide to move away you suddenly switch on to the opposite tack. At home, concentrate on creating the most tasteful and elegant atmosphere. You need calmness, preferably one filled with relaxing music, good movies on video and plenty of treats.

7 SUNDAY The Moon moves into airy Gemini today and you may experience difficulties in communicating in person with other people, particularly your friends and relations. Instead of avoiding them for fear of upsetting or antagonizing them, make an effort to see and understand their point of view. You know it will be better for all concerned in the long run.

8 MONDAY Today a Full Moon rises in the airy sign of Gemini. It would probably be a good idea if you hang on to your possessions and cash today, as well as avoiding the temptations of glitzy shops, because otherwise you may end up very much the poorer. There is also the possibility of falling out with someone close to you.

9 TUESDAY You're good at forming useful associations. Someone is keen to help you out with a project that's already taken too much of your time. You're in danger of clutching at straws, however. Go over your details once more and make sure you're not reading into a situation more than really exists.

10 WEDNESDAY Today could be a confusing time because the stars are extremely busy, so one minute you're up, the next minute you're down. During the morning workmates or loved ones may be helpful, but during the afternoon and the evening they may be deliberately aggravating or out of sorts.

The best thing you can do is get yourself into an adaptable frame of mind, or take an early night.

11 THURSDAY Family affairs are moving in a different league. The stars suggest that others will be slightly dazed and confused, and will need time to think. You, on the other hand, are in the mood for instant decisions and impulse buys. Doing what you want, your own way and in your own good time is a great tonic.

12 FRIDAY Complex situations or the way other people behave could disillusion you, but don't let this keep you from making an effort when the opportunity comes to you. In some cases conflicts give you a chance to clear up confusion, in others they settle issues of a domestic nature.

13 SATURDAY You have talents and resources, but you are unsure what to do next. There's no point making a move until you know exactly where you should be heading. Try seeking guidance. It sometimes takes another pair of eyes to see something that's been in front of your nose all along.

14 SUNDAY There may be a brand new cycle starting in your life or somebody you are financially dependent upon, whether it's a partner or a boss. Either way, you're going to gain indirectly. It's quite likely, too, that something new will enter your life, perhaps a new hobby.

15 MONDAY Ironically in at least one instance, exchanges transform previously tense situations and could even bring closer personal ties, which can't be bad. While cash matters cannot be forgotten completely, decide nothing until a few

♉

days have passed, as dramatic developments are more than you can take for the time being.

16 TUESDAY A loved one may be tired of playing guessing games, so why not give a full explanation of your movements and actions? It's a sure way to scotch any rumours concerning your behaviour. You have decisions to make and actions to take. It's a time to cut through all the gossip, petty politics and foolish pranks.

17 WEDNESDAY There seems to be a deal of emphasis on cash matters on this particular day. You may have a financial decision to make, but this is far from an ideal time for doing so. Instead, turn your attention to other things, and in the meantime make sure you don't overspend.

18 THURSDAY Because you have done so much for others, they forget that you might welcome some backing on occasions, and that is exactly what you're hoping for soon. It's important to adopt the right frame of mind. Don't be too proud to ask for help from people who you know can take something on a stage.

19 FRIDAY You're inclined to be impatient and short-tempered today when you're dealing with intense personal problems. Avoid a tendency to use material issues as a weapon. Remain open-minded in your approach otherwise you could well become involved in unnecessary conflict.

20 SATURDAY Not everyone has your instinct for what's right and what's wrong. The stars should make you determined to help others get their just desserts. No one expects you to stick your neck out, but if you don't your conscience may get the better of you. However, if you do, there'll be plenty of reason for celebration.

21 SUNDAY Even if you have big ideas and they are fool-proof, plans can go wrong, especially if someone is working against you. You must have realized now that it's not enough just to investigate problems and difficulties. You must also discover their source so the appropriate action can be taken to see that it doesn't happen again.

22 MONDAY If you're making any important decisions about the future try not to let sentiment get in the way. Old habits die hard with you, it would be the easiest thing in the world to keep things as they are. You are seen by many to be a guiding light. Once you make a break with the past others will have confidence in you.

23 TUESDAY This is the day of the New Moon and it occurs in the earthy sign of Capricorn. Matters relating to higher education, legal affairs and travel are all very well starred, so push ahead in these areas with confidence. You can't go wrong. If you are thinking of booking a holiday for next year, you couldn't pick a better time.

24 WEDNESDAY The planets suggest that today you should have plenty of energy and get-up-and-go, which is just as well since you are bound to have left some Christmas preparations until the last moment. Just remember not to try and boss others around just because you expect them to be as bright as you are. It takes all sorts to make a world.

♉

25 THURSDAY HAPPY CHRISTMAS. And it should be a good one for you because the Moon is in an earth sign. It keeps filling you with warmth and the desire to please other people – how very nice. Mind you, don't do the usual thing – over-eating or too much drinking will leave you feeling queasy for the rest of the year and that would be a shame.

26 FRIDAY After the rush and tearing about of yesterday you feel much more at ease and guests seem to be popping in, even if they're not staying very long, possibly with presents, which delights you.

27 SATURDAY This is a good time for sporting activities, and if you're going to see your favourite team play, or something similar, you're likely to be on the winning side. Those of you at home will be busy clearing up the mess after the Christmas holiday!

28 SUNDAY The Moon has now moved into the watery sign of Pisces, gingering up your social life no end. Over the next couple of days you should make a particular effort to get out and meet new people. It may well be that you run into someone who will turn out to be very special in your life. There is also likely to be a lot of activity and gossip where your existing friends are concerned. Don't take this too seriously or get it out of proportion.

29 MONDAY Sometimes you need to learn to rely on your instincts when you find yourself in puzzling situations. You tend to have a practical outlook and use your common sense, but there are times when it is better to listen to those

♉

illuminating hunches of yours. Remember, it may be that other people are puzzled and bemused as well by surprising turns of events, so it may be for you to take the lead or show the way.

30 TUESDAY If you feel you are stuck in a rut, you have nobody to blame but yourself. Meanwhile, the planets will provide you with the chance to strike a deal that you turned your back on the first time around. Take a risk and you'll open doors most people aren't even aware of; do nothing and the opportunity will disappear.

31 WEDNESDAY Well, that's the end of another year, and in the main I think it should have been a pretty good one for you. On this last day of the month it's likely that you're going to be inundated with chances for having fun and really you should decide what you want to do according to your state of health. If you're feeling jaded and generally out of sorts, then for heaven's sake just rest up at home and make phone calls. If, on the other hand, you're full of verve and enthusiasm, then get out into the big wide world and enjoy yourself.

HAPPY NEW YEAR

♉

Your Birth Chart
by
Teri King

Simply fill in your details on the form below for an interpretation of your Birth Chart by TERI KING. Your birth chart will
be supplied bound and personalized.

Each chart costs £35.00 Sterling – add £2.50 Sterling for
postage if you live outside the UK (US Dollars are not
accepted). Cheques should be made payable to *Kingstar* and
sent together with your form to: 6 Elm Grove Road, Barnes,
London SW13 0BT, England. For all *Kingstar* enquiries contact
bright77_@hotmail.com.

Date of Birth _____ Place of Birth _____

Time of Birth _____

Country of Birth _____

Name (in BLOCK CAPITALS) _____

Address _____

_____

_____ Postcode _____

Email _____

A birth chart makes an ideal present. On a separate sheet,
why not include the details of a friend, partner or a member
of your family? Please see the above costs for each individual
chart.

Your Personal Horoscope
for 2003

The only one-volume horoscope you'll ever need

Joseph Polansky

The only horoscope guide you will ever need to know about your personal horoscope for 2003. Be prepared for the future by reading Joseph Polansky's predictions for your year ahead and discover how you, your family, friends and lovers will fare. This book contains:

- a personality profile for each sign
- what you can expect in terms of wealth, home, social and love life
- a month-by-month forecast of your best days, worst days – and the ideal days for you to attract love and money.

Your Chinese Horoscope
for 2003

What the Year of the Goat holds in store for you

Neil Somerville

Learn how the Chinese Year of the Goat will affect you. This complete guide contains all the predictions you will need to help take you into the exciting new Year of the Goat. Discover how you can benefit from the year ahead – a year that offers great hope, advancement and opportunity.

This bestselling guide includes:

- an introduction to the 12 signs of the Chinese zodiac
- an explanation of the Five Elements and which govern your sign
- individual predictions to help you find love, luck and success.

Thorsons
Directions for Life

This online sanctuary is packed with information, inspiration and guidance to help you on the path to physical and spiritual well-being. Drawing on the integrity and vision of our authors and titles, and with health advice, articles, astrology, tarot, a meditation zone, author interviews and events listings, Thorsons.com is a great alternative to help create space and peace in our lives.

So if you've always wondered about practising yoga, following an allergy-free diet, using the tarot or getting a life coach, we can point you in the right direction.

Make www.thorsons.com your online sanctuary.

www.thorsons.com